Published by Paul Dilger, web www.jackbook20.com,
email paul@jackbook20.com, twitter @jackbook20, instagram jackbook20

A CIO catalogue record for this title is available from the British Library.

ISBN 978-1-8380052-0-7

you don't know jack!

WHY THE 'JACK OF ALL TRADES' TRIUMPHS IN THE MODERN WORLD

To Mary, the Portershed
and all the specialised generalists
out there.
I hope you enjoy the book.

Paul Dilger

about the author

Paul Dilger is a Jack of marketing, sales, communications, content, volunteering, racquet sports and writing. He considers himself a master of none of them. He is a keen sports player and fan. Paul prefers reading books that are putdownable. He is unashamedly middle aged, married with children and currently spends most of his time in Ireland.

He is a Master of Arts from the University of Cambridge and a Master of Business Administration from the University of Cincinnati. He is a master of neither. He still hasn't found what he's looking for, but the search goes on. He's doing it for the journey.

JACK

"*Jack of all trades, master of none*", said about someone who is able to do many things, but is not an expert in any.

Source: Cambridge Dictionary

[http://dictionary.cambridge.org/dictionary/english/jack-of-all-trades-master-of-none]

This book seeks to overcome the confusion and misplaced frustration about being not too bad at lots of things but stellar at none. It explains why the 'JOAT' should rejoice in how they are put together and celebrate it every day. It provides a way forward that is free of envy, jealousy and time-wasting, energy-sapping, wishful thinking.

"Detail of a grave featuring the Stafford Knot, Castle Church, Stafford. From Wikipedia: "The Stafford knot, sometimes incorrectly referred to as the Staffordshire knot, is a distinctive three-looped knot that is the traditional symbol of the English county" by Wiebke is licensed under CC BY 2.0

introduction

I wrestled with the structure for this book. It has three different themes, I liked them all, so I put them all in. It's classic JOAT behaviour.

The main theme of this book rationalises and celebrates us, the Jacks of All Trades*. It's a book I've designed for you to pick up and put down without losing the flow.

This book is partly autobiographical. It charts some of the main milestones in my own life and illustrates where the twists and turns have taken me away from the narrow and specialised and towards the broad and general. They appear in roughly chronological order every few pages.

It turns out that 'Jack of All Trades, Master of None' is a phrase not confined to the English language. Indeed, you can find its equivalents in many different tongues. They're peppered throughout the book to emphasise how we're encouraged to take a dim view of the JOAT across different cultures of the world. Resist that attempt to give us an inferiority complex, it's unwarranted.

** For every Jack of All Trades, there is of course a Jackie – and a Jacquie – too. After this page I almost always use the term 'JOAT' that I've coined for this book. I assure you that I'm thinking of both genders, as well as those people who don't identify with a specific gender, when I write the 'J'.*

the 99%

This book is for 99% of us.

This book is for the 99% of us you don't see on screen, you don't hear about on the radio, you don't read about in the papers.

Who are we? We are the JOATs. We're pretty good at a bunch of things, but not so good at one of them that you would know of us.

Yes, we work, we play sports, we do a bit of music, we talk politics. But we're not the 1%.

We are the people who put other people in power. We are the audiences at sports, music and other cultural events. We are the powerhouse of the organisation that gets things done. We are the buyers and consumers of things and ideas. We are the economic provider for the rich and famous.

We are the unsung heroes. We are the people that matter. We are multi-talented, we have options, and we have control. This book helps us understand why this is so and how we can live to our fullest potential.

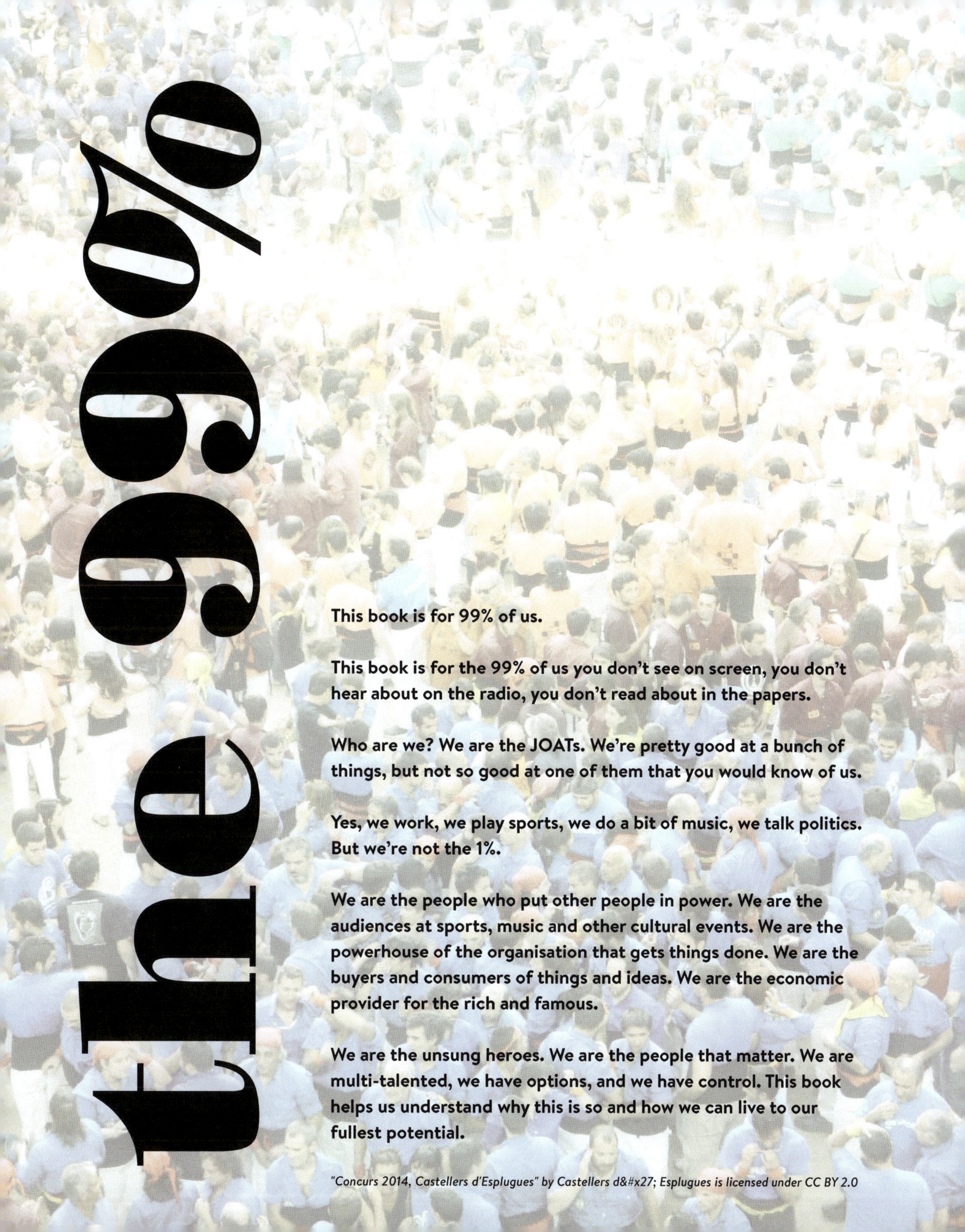

the JOAT

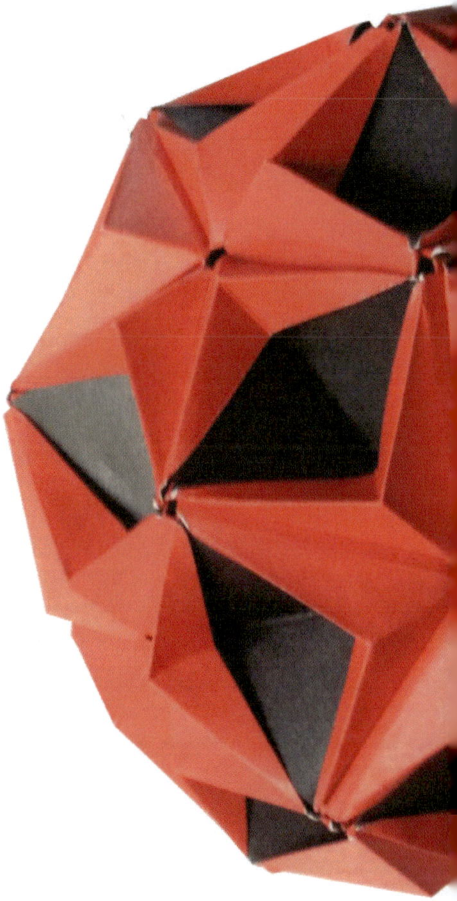

I think it's important to define what I mean by the term JOAT in this book.

A JOAT is someone who can do a number of things quite well, rather than one thing brilliantly well. These things can apply to the JOAT's working life, their hobbies, sports and pastimes, or their nearest and dearest.

As such, it also signifies their philosophies and values, how they approach their lives, how they see their place in the world.

My definition is broad because it applies to so many of us. We have breadth and some depth. We generalise a lot and we seldom specialise.

JOATs don't make the headlines. We make the world we live in, but we don't shape it, and that's absolutely fine with us.

"Starball" by Tyler Spaeth is licensed under CC BY 2.0

defined

WHAT IS THE JOAT?

What's the JOAT like? Is there a typical JOAT profile? No, but there are common elements that bind us. Each of us has reasons to be cheerful, starting with...

The JOAT can be happy. JOATs live a varied life and have a balance between the elements of their life.

The JOAT is in control. The JOAT's locus of control is internal. They understand that they have the power to make things happen. Sure, things may happen to them occasionally, but the JOAT knows that they have the power to effect change for themselves and others.

The JOAT is flexible. The JOAT's inherent adaptability means they can go either way. The JOAT's inherent mobility means that they're never in a rut long enough to get stuck.

The JOAT is free. The JOAT always has options and these options are what give the JOAT control. Freedom comes from being able to make choices.

The JOAT is lucky. The JOAT knows hard work and dedication will result in more good breaks than bad breaks. The JOAT makes luck. The JOAT manages luck.

The JOAT is realistic. Realism is often confused with pessimism, since these days people feel they have to be irrepressibly optimistic. The JOAT hopes for the best and plans for the worst. The JOAT always has a plan B. The JOAT knows that things never work out exactly as planned.

The JOAT is good. Regardless of their religious or spiritual leanings, the JOAT understands the essence of being a good person, a good citizen, a good human being.

"Jack of All Trades 1900 by JJ Bell + illustr. by C. Robinson" by Paul K is licensed under CC BY 2.0

early school years

My primary school and early secondary school education was a blur of different subjects and activities. I suspect it was the same for most people. I was educated back in the 1970s and I'm not sure if the fundamentals have changed much since then. Education's role for this age group is a case of exposing the child to a range of different experiences so that they start to find stuff they like and stuff they're good at. This has the effect of producing fairly well-rounded citizens who can function in a modern society and do the basic things that are expected of our higher order species.

I was reasonably good at all sports, playing football, rugby, cricket, rounders, athletics, basketball, table tennis, tennis, badminton, swimming, darts and snooker. I was not reasonably good at things where my feet had reduced friction with the ground, such as ice skating, roller-skating and skateboarding. The only sport I was never really exposed to was martial arts in its various forms.

I was also a cub scout from the age of eight to eleven, and therefore received lessons in life skills like knotting, camping, map-reading, leading younger cub scouts, that kind of thing. There was a certain institutional and Victorian feel to be being a cub scout back then, in that you were being moulded into accepting authority, respecting elders and knowing your place in the hierarchy.

I was also lucky enough to be academically decent too, so I got to go the local grammar school and study languages like Latin and Greek, in addition to the usual fodder. In other words, I had the typical JOAT upbringing. Variety was set down early as the spice of life.

Nineteenth century woodcut of a mother and daughter in a confectioner's shop (candy store), probably from the decade of the 1810s. The girl is wearing pantalettes. This work is in the public domain in its country of origin and other countries and areas where the copyright term is the author's life plus 70 years or less.

كتير الكارات، قليل البارات

("Who does several trades, is incapable of managing any")

Syrian Arabic

"Jack of all trades (60-ies)." by Ion Chibzii is licensed under CC BY-SA 2.0

File:Neoltwigi.jpg (category Seesaws in South Korea) English Neolttwigi game around 1905. This work is in the public domain in its country of origin and other countries and areas where the copyright term is the author's life plus 70 years or less.

why the JOAT should read this book

You're a so-called generalist, pigeon-holed and saddled with monikers like 'jack of all trades', 'all-rounder', or even 'team player'.

Perhaps you detect a prevailing view that being quite good at a lot of things is somehow a bad thing, a feeling often held by JOATs themselves.

Read this book to correct the balance.

You know who you are and you know what you can do. It's about time others knew too.

WHO IS THE JOAT?

The JOAT craves variety.

The JOAT delights in diversity.

The JOAT is comforted by a little bit of everything.

The JOAT is adaptable.

The JOAT is an 'outside-in person'. The JOAT wants to understand the whole picture before they drill into the detail.

The JOAT loves context. Anything in isolation is anathema to the JOAT.

The JOAT is about the sum of the parts, which is greater than the whole.

The JOAT wants to know how the pieces fit together, what the links in the chain are from end to end.

The JOAT gets bored quickly.

The JOAT doesn't like to be idle.

The JOAT isn't comfortable with a lack of flexibility, freedom or options.

The JOAT is wary of focusing too much, of getting too deep.

The JOAT doesn't like to pick one thing, to put it all on red, to gamble on the eggs in the one basket.

The JOAT sees a gap in the market, but worries if there's a market in the gap.

The JOAT is you.

WHAT DOES THE JOAT DO?

The JOAT gets it done. Time is precious and you can't get back wasted or lost time. Want something done? Get it to the JOAT.

The JOAT is quick to thank. The JOAT acknowledges the help and contribution of others. The JOAT is grateful for the time other people put aside for them.

The JOAT is a giver. The JOAT shares information, reveals the short cut, exposes the insight. A problem shared is a problem halved, but for the JOAT a solution shared is a benefit doubled.

The JOAT pays it forward. The JOAT repays the kindness and indulgence of others by doing the same to others, so that the ripple of human kindness expands.

The JOAT picks a card and puts one down. The JOAT is always looking to improve the hand of cards they have. They try something new, consider the set, and discard the weakest.

The JOAT avoids unproductive feelings. The JOAT is all about productivity, since it is a function of time. Feelings like guilt and envy are unwanted because they eat away at you and eat away at your productive time.

The JOAT lives in the present, with an eye to the future. For the JOAT, the past is done, and the lessons are learned. The JOAT's future helps shape their present.

The JOAT knows the destination, but understands the route is not clear. The JOAT drives in the direction of the headlights, and adjusts accordingly.

The JOAT is active, physical and moving. The JOAT abhors inertia, indecision and incapacity.

Do you recognise yourself in some of this? It's what we JOATs do.

a collection of school jobs

What is the collective noun for jobs? A litany, or even an infestation, if we have too many of them. In keeping with my generalist approach to life so far, I held a number of different jobs and pastimes while at school.

My first ever job, apart from the chores of cleaning my room and polishing my shoes for pocket money, was a newspaper round. Seven days of getting up at the crack of dawn for the princely sum of £2.60 per week. This was 1979, the heyday for the fourth estate and newspapers were big, very big. On a Friday the weekly local paper came out, and it was a monster. Imagine tottering out on your bike in the pitch dark with a 20-pound bag over each shoulder, in the worst winter for decades, when the snow and ice still hadn't lifted by the end of March. I soon ditched the bike in favour of walking round. You still nearly passed out because the straps cut off all blood flow around your collar bone, but it beat coming off the bike every ten yards.

Pretty soon I graduated to working in the newsagent's, selling all and sundry and doing the adding up and the change in my head rather than using the till, to improve my numeracy. I also played a lot of darts in the back of the shop, which is also very good for your sums. During my last two years of school I got involved in my first taste of administration, paying back the years of table tennis coaching by serving as secretary of my county's league. I still had no idea what to do in life, but I was accumulating a range of experiences.

"Dewey Defeats Truman" by David Erickson is licensed under CC BY 2.0

周身刀,無張利

("Equipped with knives all over, yet none is sharp")

Cantonese

THE JOAT AND THE GENERALIST

Is there a difference between the terms JOAT and generalist? JOAT has almost always been used as a pejorative term suggesting mediocrity, as if being able to do a bunch of things was somehow bad.

These days people tend to use the term generalist. It sounds fancier, more positive somehow. It also tends to be used by people who either are generalists themselves or want to increase the stock of the JOAT.

Of course, as you can tell from the industrial word 'trade', the term pre-dates us all by quite some way. Correspondingly, the fortunes of the JOAT have ebbed and flowed over the generations. In the pre-Internet era a generalist background was considered the best background for the well-rounded business person. Even though the Internet is simply the delivery mechanism, it has been responsible for an astonishingly quick shift in opportunity, access and competition for all.

This has resulted in the business world maturing extremely quickly and the last two decades has seen the balance move firmly in favour of the specialist. All is not lost for the generalist, however, since the roles of CEO/Chief Executive and entrepreneur/owner-manager are much more suited to those people with a decent command of all the business areas.

But what about those of us who are not CEO or entrepreneur material, at least not yet? We tend to use JOAT as a self-deprecatory way of describing our skill-set. In this sense we do ourselves a disservice.

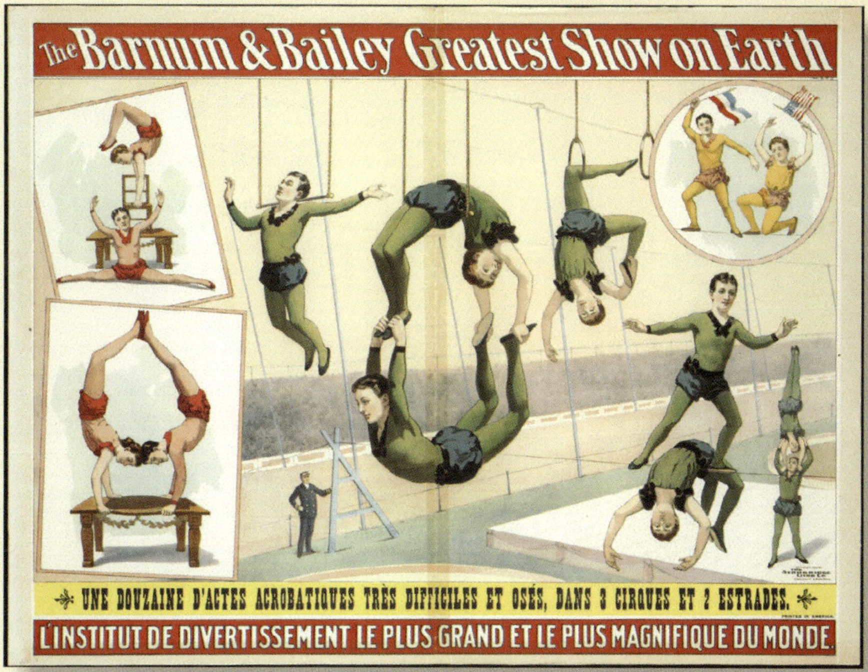

"The Barnum & Bailey greatest show on earth : L'Institut de divertissement le plus grand et le plus magnifique du monde." by Boston Public Library is licensed under CC BY 2.0

all hail the mistake maker

“Award-wining photographer and journalist”, “successful track record of delivering results above targets”, “former grand slam winner and world no.1”. We all want to be associated with these people. We feel safe and comfortable hiring successful people. Their track record is something we hope they will bring to us and something we can hide behind if things go awry. “Well, I picked the best, don’t blame me.”

It’s all nonsense. You know it is, right? Any profile, bio or CV is necessarily selective, and it’s no surprise that the high points are selected and presented in the best light. The failures are conveniently omitted from the narrative, and downplayed if they come up in conversation. When was the last time someone described themselves as “award-losing writer”, “target-missing sales manager”, or “mistake-maker and perennial promotion bridesmaid”? It’s not in our nature is it? The truth is this: it’s the mistakes that make us. The lessons we learn are the prized assets in a person. “I tried and failed at this. I know the pitfalls and the banana skins and I can help you avoid them.”

JOATs know a thing or two about making mistakes and not winning. We’re making them all the time, because we’re working on a lot of things and we’re not masters at any of them. Fear of failing is one thing, but a culture of accepting failure and moving on stronger from it is another thing entirely. We salute the mistake-making generalists. They don’t make the same mistake twice, they present a moving target to the world and they’re getting things done. If you’re not making mistakes, one of two things is happening. Either you’re not moving fast enough, or you’re not pushing yourself.

altitude sickness in the

high-flying company

It's hard not to feel a tinge of envy at the individuals of the company that sells out for millions or billions, netting the founders and investors vast fortunes in the process. "If only I'd got in there, strapped myself to the rocket ship. I could have been somebody. Who knew they'd be the one?"

These are one-in-a-thousand success stories, but they are amplified to such an extent that they seem more commonplace. They hide the dizzying numbers of companies that simply bob along the surface, not doing that much in relative terms, except satisfying their customers and providing a livelihood for their staff. They're also silent on the 'back story' of what the protagonists had to go through to get where they did.

The question is this: in a high-flying company can you have people who are less than brilliant? Is each person in each role brilliant, from the CEO down? Do they seek out the most stellar receptionist money can buy? Do all the masters of their own trade get altitude sickness in that rarified atmosphere of brilliance?

And are the JOATs not the glue that keeps the company together, using their superior interpersonal and boundary-spanning management skills to keep the company in the fastest-moving part of the river and make sure there's no fire on board or treacherous waterfall in the distance?

'ordinary' arts and sciences

There is an unending debate about which country's education system is better: the one that gets you to specialise early, or the one that gives you more time. Do you specialise after your first major exams at age sixteen, or when you get to college, or even after your first degree, moving onto a Master's or PhD?

In the middle England of the 1980s - I use the term geographically rather than socio-politically - we took our 'Ordinary Levels' at age sixteen. These 'O' Levels were fairly major exams that determined to a large extent which three or four subjects we would take on to advanced level, unless we opted for leaving school at sixteen to pursue a trade, which at the time was what a sizeable proportion of kids did. This meant that by age thirteen we had already started to specialise in some areas and defocus from others.

In addition to the compulsory subjects like English writing, literature and mathematics, I opted for what I considered to be 'heavyweight' subjects in the arts and sciences. I dropped practical subjects like metal work and wood work since I hated them and had almost zero ability. I also dropped the social sciences which I had already decided didn't do much for me. The casualties on the way, that I would never study again, were the 'works', technical drawing, history, geography and biology.

That left me with my core eight subjects of English, English Lit, Maths, French, Latin, Greek, Physics and Chemistry. The early bias towards languages and a love of language was there - and some would say at this point I was in danger of becoming a Jack of All Languages - but there was a good spattering of numeracy and the scientific as well, to round out the balance.

"The Ordinary Tavern" by ikrichter is licensed under CC BY 2.0

Katica za sve

("Kate for everything")

Croatian

"Kate Moss Brainwashed" by bixentro is licensed under CC BY 2.0

are we following the

Who are our role models? Whose posters adorned the walls of our bedrooms when we were growing up? Film and TV stars? Music stars? Pop stars? Sporting heroes? Fighting heroes? Sex gods and goddesses? Cartoon or comic book characters? Business icons? Entrepreneurs? World leaders?

Do we look to them for inspiration? Or do we strive to be like them, to take their place? And what happens next year when their star fades, and we lose interest in them, and their posters are replaced by those of the new gods, the new heroes? They're still doing what they do best, aren't they? They haven't changed their tune, tried something else, started again, like we have.

These are unattainable dreams, to all but the very few who knew from very early on that

wrong role models?

this is what they were born to do, what they wanted to do. They have one dimension, one direction, one dream. We don't.

Who ever had a poster of their parents made and put up on a wall? The people who spent their adult lives helping to make us the people we are today? Who scrimped and saved, sweated and worried for us? Who we have to thank for putting up with us? Who we took for granted as we got older and who we wish we'd done more for now they're gone? Who, actually, we strive to be like, kind of?

They're in the photo frames on our table, but why aren't they in the posters on our walls? And why not our teachers, coaches, mentors too?

THE COP OUT

The main criticism you'll run into with the central argument of this book is this: it's a cop out. It gives people a reason to give up, an excuse for not being good enough, so that they can explain away their mediocrity. After all, it's the perfect alibi, isn't it?

"This is an average book, written by an average guy, for average people. It stops you chasing your dreams, it suffocates ambition. No-one ever got anywhere by being average."

This is of course partly true. Perhaps it is an average book. But I'm not average, and neither are you as you read this. The average anything is an artificial construct, a mathematical nicety that we use as a guide to explain things and give us the shortcut to navigating through the complexity of life.

I know, I could have written the book better. I could have introduced the concept more eloquently. But the ideas in this book are new, they are different, and they've been living out in the wide open, staring us in the face for as long as we've stood up on two legs.

We have the choice. We have the control. We're consciously choosing this path because it gives us options, and it gives us enjoyment. No-one can tell us otherwise.

We're not copping out. To coin a phrase much loved by the people of both Liverpool and Ireland: we're copping on.

"Avoid Cerebral Incursions" by CaptMikey9 is licensed under CC BY 2.0

the grass is always greener

"How did she manage to get that great job? I never rated her that highly."

"I can't believe they chose him for that part ahead of me. What does he have that I don't?"

It's very hard not to let the green-eyed monster escape every so often. We JOATs feel this very keenly. We can do lots of things pretty well, but often it seems our best in one thing is not good enough to nail the big one. It seems that somewhere the grass is always greener.

MY SIDE

THE OTHER SIDE

But do you know what? These guys that we look up to, admire, envy? They have their problems too. They see greener grass in someone else's garden too. The rich will always want to get richer, comparing themselves to others on the rich list. The powerful want to get more powerful, and plot to increase their power base and influence at the expense of others trying to do the same to them. The famous want to become more famous, addicted to the narcotic forces of publicity.

The grass always seems greener, but that's almost never the case. When we move from one job to the next, one company to the next, one challenge to the next, we simply inherit a different set of challenges, and a different set of easier things and harder things.

We JOATs recognise this and we embrace it, because if there's one thing that should make us happy, it's different stuff.

advancing to languages

After taking my eight Ordinary Levels, I needed to pick four subjects for Advanced Level, or 'A' Level for short. One of the A Levels was General Studies which the school picked for us and consisted of weekly lessons about current affairs and the world at large, for the classic JOAT 'rounding' A Level. I imagine the idea was to prepare us for life outside the cocoon of the family, since many of us would be heading away to some form of third level education.

At my school they laid on extra classes so that we could get a taster of what was to come in A Level. I had received good grades in my Maths and Physics 'O' Levels, but the stuff we did in those six weeks, which was meant to be a gradual transition to the harder stuff, scared the living daylights out of me. I decided that I wanted to continue my love affair with languages. My remaining three A Levels were therefore an easy choice. Latin, Greek and French made up the quartet.

Except, not quite. I had little or no interest in current affairs at that time, and there was an option to slot in an extra subject and simply turn up on the day and take the General Studies exam 'blind'. What more excuse did I need to add another trade to my armoury? I decided to do Russian O Level alongside my four A levels, thereby generalising across a range of tongues which spanned an entire continent and two-and-a-half millennia.

123
OPEN SESAME
TAKALANI SESAME

Devatero řemesel, desátá bída.

("Nine crafts, tenth is misery")

Czech

"Tools" by Steve Snodgrass is licensed under CC BY 2.0

what do you want to do in life?

What do you want to do in life? Is this a question you've always struggled with? It's funny how this question always seems to have a career-based or vocation-based slant to it.

"I want to be an Olympic champion at the 400-metre hurdles."

"I want to start my own business making a new type of widget."

"I want to become the minister for the arts."

"I want to run an independent cinema."

"I want to help orphans in the Sudan."

These are all laudable goals, but they're all vocational. Of course, you have the other extreme as well.

"I want to do as little as possible to get by."

"I want to sell drugs."

"I want to control an illegal operation."

There are doubtless JOATs who are plying trades which are at the expense of other people and outside the normal parameters of society. These people do not believe in the fair exchange, and this book is not for them.

You hardly ever hear any avocational answers which are directed to family, friends or free time.

"I want to be a well-rounded parent to my kids so that they can sample a range of experiences and choose the ones that make them tick."

"I want to be there for my parents and my older siblings when they need me."

"I want to spend my evenings teaching my friends how to knit."

"I want people to feel that leisure time spent with me is time well spent."

jack of many trades

jack of many trades

The funny thing about the phrase 'jack of all trades, master of none' is that we don't take it literally. We don't really mean someone can become competent in all trades and get fairly good at everything. That's not possible. You can see why other languages have developed similar phrases with a specific number of trades in them, which seems a far more realistic and succinct way of explaining people's bias against the generalist.

The JOAT definition I offered at the beginning of this book focussed on being able to do many things, to be a jack of many trades. How many is many though? It's more than one, certainly, but is it a couple, a few, several, or plain old many? I've adopted a broad interpretation of many, because the topic itself is broad and therefore the ideas in this book will be useful to more people. In short, useful to the 99% of us.

How many trades? Between three and seven, most of the time, in my view.

When I think of the word 'trade', I don't confine my thinking to the working world. It's a capability that belongs both inside and outside of work, and applies to our interactions with family, friends and colleagues before 9am, from 9 to 5, and after 5pm. Our skillset is for both work and play.

When we take this holistic approach to being a JOAT, which addresses both work and non-work skills, it better serves our efforts to become well-rounded individuals. After all, we might act differently at work, but we're still the same 'whole' person at work or play, and it's the sum of our trades that characterises our whole.

WINNERS COME SECOND

It takes a certain kind of ruthlessness to come first. You have to be single-minded and put yourself before everyone and everything else.

We all come across certain types of 'winners' in our working and playing lives. They almost never have a trace of humility. In some quarters you might call them bullies. They're the sort of person who views coming second as 'first loser'. As far as they're concerned, those who don't come first lack that killer instinct. Not being able to get the job done is a cop out in their eyes.

JOATs don't have that singled-minded streak of ruthlessness. That's not how we're wired. At heart we should be happy, settled people who have an equilibrium in our life. We understand the importance of balance for longevity.

When I was eighteen and looking at universities I came across the Oxford University Alternative Prospectus, written by students – brilliantly written I might add. It was designed as an antidote to the stuffiness of the official prospectus and gave you an insight into what college life was really like. I remember one page was entitled "Why You Should Not Go for a First" – a first being a first-class degree, the top echelon of results.

It focused on all the other important experiences going to college would present to you, apart from the obvious academic one. It talked about the abundance and variety of facets of college life, all of which should be sampled. In short, it was a manifesto for the JOAT. Oxford graduates who don't get firsts and leave academia seem to do OK, don't they?

a sporting life

Are you an individual sports person, or a team sports person? I, as you might expect, have a foot in both camps. I've had most success in individual sports, specifically racquet sports. It takes a lot of time and effort to rack up the thousands of hours you need to be considered an expert in something, so the sports I did more of, I got better at. I played table tennis to the point where I was ranked in England at the under-seventeen age group. I was school champion at tennis, and club standard, but not anywhere near the same level as my table tennis. I was proficient at squash, badminton, and racquetball, but nothing more. I tried watersports, frisbee and a host of other sports once, and for me once was enough, I wasn't hooked.

I also spent a lot of time doing things that were typically viewed as the product of a mis-spent youth. Hours and hours of darts in the back of the newsagent's or in the school common room, and lots of snooker on small tables added to my general hand-to-eye co-ordination. As I got older I started going on the occasional ski holiday, but I wouldn't call myself proficient.

Then there are the team sports. I played football, rugby, field hockey and cricket for my school, but my lack of size and raw speed was an issue. I rowed a little as a novice at college and played cricket for my first post-college employer, but found myself drifting away from organised team sport after my mid-twenties. It wasn't until my very late thirties that I rediscovered my love for football, and have played five-, six-, or seven-a-side ever since. I can't think of any sport I enjoy doing more, and it's the team counterbalance to my solo sports.

12 ambachten, 13 ongelukken

("12 trades, 13 accidents")

Dutch

Role models can form a vital function in helping us to improve. Indeed, change tends not to happen without them. We look up to role models. They inspire us to do better and show us how it's done, so we can emulate their behaviour and become better ourselves. As the moniker suggests, they provide a model for the role we're looking to fulfill ourselves.

So where are the JOAT role models? They're not famous, so they're not in the public eye and we don't see them. JOATs don't make the news. The news is only interested in people or things that are at the top of their specialty. The world is run by specialists. One of the main fears of the specialist is that they will be found out as not a master of their subject, whereas the JOAT delights in this situation. That said, the JOAT role models are out there, but where?

There is no one role for the JOAT, because each JOAT's combination of trades is unique.

WHERE ARE THE JOAT ROLE MODELS?

It follows, then, that there is no single role model for our own specific blend of skills. There are however, plenty of JOAT role models who have a different make-up to us but who can still provide an example by the nature of how they operate as individuals. They might be our parents, our siblings, or even our kids. They might be friends or acquaintances. Chances are they're behind the scenes, making the specialists look good, giving without expecting anything in return.

Be attentive, seek them out, see how they do what they do – and take their best bits that might work for you.

WHY DIDN'T I THINK OF THAT?

"Oh, that's such an obvious idea, simple really. Why has no-one thought of that? More importantly, why the blue blazes didn't I think of it?" This kind of reverse rationalising we do when we see a powerfully simple idea is deceiving. It's much harder to come up with a drinks cooler with a built-in MP3 player than you might think.

The Edison quote of genius – creating something new is 1% inspiration and 99% perspiration – still holds true. At some point in our endeavours we reach an impasse and we labour over how we can bypass it or create something to bypass it. "Why isn't there an X to do Y?" It's from our efforts that we spot a gap in our thinking, a niche we can occupy, or a way to help ourselves or help others.

I used to work for a guy who said, "when I was trying to set up my previous business, there was no service provider focused on providing everything technological a small business would need to run their business: networking, connectivity, hosting, storage, email, web, security. So I started one." It seemed obvious at the time but no-one had done it. He did it, and did very well too.

Coming up with a great idea is not the private domain of geniuses, the gifted and the specialists. It's for you and me too. We are JOATs who acquire experiences for breakfast, it's what we do. And you know what? The idea is only a tiny part of it. The idea won't blossom into something real without dedication, hard work, and the grasp of a broad set of skills. And do you know who has those skills in spades? Yep, we do.

"d'oh digital me02" by everythingis-blooming is licensed under CC BY 2.0

you are not average

You're not an average person. None of the things you do is average.

Average is a mathematical concept. It doesn't exist. Take a group of people or a group of numbers. 'Mode' is the most common element in the group, and 'median' is the middle element in the group when the numbers or people are arranged in order. They exist. Average is the total of the group divided by the number in the group. Like I said, it doesn't exist in real life.

Average is like a stereotype, or a persona. It's a collection of traits that come together to form an approximation of some people, but not one person. It's a guide for other people or organisations to box us up, define us and communicate with us as economically as possible. What it should never be is a standard by which we define ourselves.

The trouble with statistics is that they're a guide to a group of things or people, but not to an individual. Just because the average exam mark is 57% doesn't mean that you'll probably score about 57%. Just because the average temperature in southern Spain is thirty-two degrees in August doesn't mean it will be that when you go in August. Just because the average JOAT is a Jack or Jackie of five trades doesn't mean five is the right number for you.

Resist the urge to consider yourself average. You aren't.

the three-pronged spear of work experience

I got offers to go to University after A levels, but not from the University I really wanted. I tried to get into Oxford University. The two Oxbridge establishments had their own entrance exams the autumn term before A levels. I was quite young for my academic year, had no connections to Oxford, and wasn't good enough. After my A levels I opted to stay on an extra autumn term to try and get into Cambridge University, using what few connections and history our school had had with the august establishment.

I got in, but this left me with eight months to kill before going up to college the following autumn. I looked around, with my Dad's help, for useful experiences to keep me busy and learn something of the world before getting back into education. We found a small voluntary organisation who ran a scheme called project Trident, hence the three prongs. It was manna from heaven for the generalist: six months' work experience, a month's expedition, two weeks' voluntary work in a disabled holiday home. Sorted!

Kiu ĉasas du leporojn, kaptas neniun.

("Who chases two jackrabbits catches none")

Esperanto

we are all JOATs

When we watch great dancers in action, we marvel at their skill and imagine what it must be like to be in their shoes. Being at the top of your industry, with the exception of a few industries, can happen for a fleetingly short time, so we can't begrudge these people their moment in the sun. After all, they've worked impossibly hard and sacrificed a ton of things to get there.

After they've retired from the performing arts, if they've anything between their ears they tend to go into management, coaching, writing or broadcasting about their beloved art form. They use their knowledge and experience from their first specialism to ease as smoothly as they can into a related specialism. Most of the acknowledged greats of broadcasting and writing didn't do much, if anything, in the arts or sports themselves, yet they are masters of this form of communication.

We are all JOATs and it depends on how we define and segment the term 'trade'. There are well-known experts in social media, but their expertise is typically around one of the platforms, such as Facebook. If they are acknowledged experts in Facebook, they might have a further specialism in how to generate traffic to your Facebook page using free methods, or they might be masters of how best to use the paid advertising options. Then there will be specialists within those options too.

The more tightly you define or sub-divide a trade, the more chance you have of being a specialist, but the harder it is to make a name and a living in that super-narrow niche. That's why in the real world we're all generalists.

THERE ARE NO MORE RENAISSANCE MEN

There are no more renaissance men or women. No more polymaths, true acknowledged masters at more than one thing. Society is not set up that way any more; it's too open and accessible for you to be number 1 in a few small 'members only' coteries.

If you're old enough, you'll remember people who represented their country at two or more sports. When I was younger I knew an older chap at the local tennis club who had played rugby for Ireland, tennis for Scotland, and hockey for Wales.

Some of you may remember Americans Bo Jackson in the 1980s and Deion Sanders in 1990s, both of whom played professional football and baseball to very high standards. Deion Sanders was also an NCAA track star, a blindingly fast athlete.

Those of you who are older still may know Jonathan Miller, who started out in Beyond the Fringe and went on to be pre-eminent in theatre, television and the arts. He was also an extremely accomplished medical man.

Of course, the term dates back to the renaissance period and birth of university education where you learned a 'universe' of subjects rather than specialising in one area.

There are no more renaissance men. The world is fairer, there is too much opportunity and too much access for one person to excel in more than one area at the very highest level. Sooner or later the master wannabe has to specialise, and if they haven't specialised early and dedicated themselves to the cause they may never get anywhere near the top of the tree.

"Yes, but your approach is to dumb everything down. You reduce the importance of everything, you trivialise it. Your make it mediocre. Your approach is wrong." So say the specialists in their field, the masters of their trade, the intellectuals in their ivory towers. These are the people who cured diseases, invented devices and appliances, explained the universe, built magnificent buildings and art, and because of whom we JOATs benefit, along with the rest of humanity, every hour of every day.

But do we run the risk of living and working a superficial existence? If we examine our lives are we painting by numbers and making judgments from snippets? Are we categorising around stereotypes and making pronouncements with sound-bites? Yes there is a risk, if we don't know ourselves and if we're not true to ourselves.

Do you think that when Mark Twain said "I didn't have time to write you a short letter, so I wrote you a long one," he was referring to dumbing down? No, of course not. It takes far more effort to come up with something simple, than something complex. It is the act of consideration and analysis of the factors – you'll never have all the information you need to make a perfect decision – that leads to the filtration of thoughts into something nugget-like, something compelling and piercing.

The JOAT doesn't need to get as deep into things and get immersed in the detail like the specialist does. The JOAT is not competing with the specialist. The JOAT is not about dumbing it down. The JOAT is about sharpening it up.

"'Mark Twain' -- Statue at Glascock's Landing on the Mississippi River Front in Hannibal (MO) May 2018" by Ron Cogswell is licensed under CC BY 2.0

a college life for me

Cambridge University is really an assortment of faculties on campuses where you go to lectures. The rest of the time, the bulk of your work and your living is decentralised into colleges.

95% of the time you belonged at college because you had exhibited some degree of prowess academically. To all but a few of us however, although we wanted to do as well as possible, this would be the end of our academic lives. Here, after all, was a place where you could potentially tread the same path as sporting superstars, brilliant thinkers and world-famous writers and comedians had trodden before you. But hold on, didn't that mean you needed to be a master already, before you could brave the harrowing auditions, the team trials and so on to become one of these elite specialists?

Sure, I wanted to play varsity tennis, I wanted to be in the Footlights, and I wanted to broadcast for the BBC, but these were all things that hitherto I had seen on the 'telly' and thought "that would be nice." Some of them needed previous years of dedication, and others didn't need dedication but oodles of natural talent and some excellent connections. I hadn't the nerve to try any of these things. I was a product of a safe, well-rounded upbringing, and this kind of fame and fortune was simply too extreme for me. So, I did my studies, captained the University table tennis team, was student union president of my college, and kept my life busy and varied. Do you see a pattern emerging here?

Üheksa ametit, kümnes nälg

("Nine trades, the tenth one — hunger")
Estonian

"Irish Hunger Memorial" by Eden, Janine and Jim is licensed under CC BY 2.0

KNOW THYSELF

NOSCE TEIPSUM.

Lady Cyclist (touring in North Holland). "WHAT A RIDICULOUS COSTUME!"

"Know thyself." So said the ancient Greek philosopher Socrates, teacher of Plato. He felt the unexamined life was not worth living and for us JOATs it's a point well made. The JOAT keeps a portfolio of skills going, and it's important for the JOAT to understand which skills and how many should be honed for a successful blend.

Just as athletes are good at listening to their bodies and spotting the leading indicators of sickness or pain, so must the JOAT constantly evaluate the set of things they're pretty good at. In my fitness life, I do a bit of running. I like to run for about half an hour, or about five or six kilometres. Something that gives me the aerobic benefits. I know my limits. I once ran eighteen miles and hated it. I know I could run a marathon if I really pushed myself, but I'm most comfortable at shorter distances. In the world of athletics it doesn't take runners very long, from the sixty-metre dash up to the ultra-marathon, to figure out what their strongest events are.

Similarly, I know I sometimes struggle with short-term memory, which might affect my productivity in all the things I do fairly well. So, I keep a day-book of key points on a call that I scribble down, and I do the same thing on my laptop in meetings. Finally, because I've worked in a few industries and am not a subject matter expert in any of them, when I'm called upon to be a subject matter expert, or 'SME' in a presentation or webinar, I research, script and deliver exactly what I'm going to say. If there are some unstructured Q&A at the end, I may ask a genuine SME to support me.

LIVE TO WORK, WORK TO LIVE

Do you live to work, or do you work to live? We've all met the person who lives to work. From the moment they wake up, to the moment they go to bed, they think about work. They seem to do little else. It occupies their every waking thought. Do they love their job? Possibly. Are they afraid of letting anything else into their lives? Possibly. Are we this person? Probably not.

The JOAT typically works to live. This is not to say that they don't give their work 100%. For the JOAT, however, there is more to life than work. Working life is the richer for the other things in it, and family life, friend life and free time life is the richer for the freedom that the working life brings. If you were independently wealthy, or had riches that removed the need to work, would you still work? What about after the novelty of the extended break wears off?

The wealthy JOAT still fills their lives with a variety of activities and occupations, albeit a different set of them than before.

Many JOATs don't know the answer to the question "what do you want to do in life?" Perhaps they still haven't found what they're looking for, they haven't found their mastery yet. What the JOAT does know is that the answer isn't merely a question about working life. That's a part of it, but only one part. JOATs keep looking, keep trying new things, keep searching. And they strive to be happy, to achieve the happiness that comes from a varied and balanced life.

The JOAT works to live. There is no shame in this. After all, all work and no play make Jack a dull boy...

being blessed

I'm not getting all spiritual on you here. I don't mean blessed by either a real person or something or someone more ethereal. I mean blessed by our DNA, the unique mix of genes we've inherited.

We JOATS, we're blessed in so many ways, we sometimes don't know it. Sometimes we treat it as a millstone rather than a trampoline. Look at all the things we can do well! Look how well we try new things! See how we're always learning, always looking to build our knowledge, our experiences, our abilities! We rock, we 99% of society!

This – the nature of being blessed with an ability to do lots of things to a decent degree – is my main excuse for taking so long to write this book. It was a major project for me, an ambitious one. It took me a long time to

marshal my thoughts, and my thinking certainly evolved over the years I was writing it. Yes, I could have written it from cover to cover in two months if I blocked out the world, but that's not in my nature. That goes against the grain of the JOAT. Besides, I had lots of other fun stuff to do.

Being blessed is not a pass to avoid being disciplined, however.

We must keep tabs on our concentration and intensity, not lapsing into a tendency to flit between things. We shouldn't spread ourselves too thin. We do lots of things well, we don't do everything poorly.

the classics - plural

At college I opted to study what is known as 'Classics'. This is called the even grander Literae Humaniores at Oxford University, but in essence they're both the same: Latin and Ancient Greek. When I was doing my degree, it didn't matter how unvocational your undergraduate degree was, so the fact that I was studying two dead languages was a non-issue. The rationale of the time still holds true, namely that they provide an excellent platform for studying the 'romance' languages and help a lot with figuring out what words mean in our adopted Anglo-Saxon tongue.

It sounds like I'm specialising quite considerably at this stage, but it's not really the case. Firstly, I was studying two languages, not one, hence the subject matter of the classics - plural. Secondly, within each language for the first part of the degree you had to immerse yourself in the literature, philosophy and the history of each language. Your score in the first part didn't carry forward at all into the second and final part, which was a blessing for me because I'm better at peaking for final exams. I was also pretty poor at both the history and the philosophy, lacking the rigour for the former and the brainpower for the latter.

For my finals, I had to take five papers. One was a general essay paper, where almost any question could come up. Another paper I chose was Latin literature. My specialty, if you can call it that, which covered the remaining three papers, was Classical Linguistics. It again covered both Latin and Greek, with a sprinkling of other languages like Sanskrit, Linear B and the purely hypothetical 'Indo-European.' Not so much deep, then, as wide.

Qui trop embrasse, mal étreint

("He who embraces too much, has a weak grasp")

French

"Lost Balloons" by Alex Lovell-Troy is licensed under CC BY 2.0

CATHOLICS, CONNOISSEURS AND CHECKS

We are JOATs. Our tastes are catholic, with a small c. Some of us might also be Catholic, with a big C, but that's not the point. Because we do lots of things, and we like lots of things, we're open-minded when it comes to stimuli. We like lots of sports, we like many different art forms. We warm to many different musical genres, movies, books, plays and shows. We're a pretty well-rounded bunch.

The French have no word for connoisseur. Actually, of course they do, just as they have a word for entrepreneur too, the quotation we erroneously attribute to a former American president. Who wants to be a connoisseur? A connoisseur is like a specialist, that gifted individual who has a responsibility to nurture that gift and constantly push the boundaries of their speciality so that we JOATs may enjoy it along with our other pursuits. Leave it to them, we've plenty of other things to experience.

The checks and balances are there to keep the system on an even keel. We JOATs are well used to having checks and balances, as we manage our portfolio of trades. I'm willing to bet that it's this balanced approach that gives us our solid moral compass. We do good and we do right. We help out, and we volunteer. If we don't do good, and we don't do what's right, then we do our fellow people, our fellow JOATs, a disservice. Immoral behaviour is not JOAT behaviour.

IN SEARCH OF THE NEW

We love variety, we JOATs. Perhaps this is why we get bored easily. Variety is the drug we thrive on. We're always looking for the new, something new to try, to add to our swelling fund of experience.

This makes us ideal people for the modern world, where life is not quite exclusively measured in 140-character soundbites, but certainly in much shorter bursts than before. Making the most of today's world is about being curious, questioning, adaptable and brave. There is no status quo to speak of. Everything is in motion all the time. If you're not moving, you're going backwards, and we have become professionally mobile.

The new and the different is what turns us on, and holds our attention, albeit fleetingly. We have become accomplished surfers, skimmers, samplers and speed-readers. We look to get the gist of something, form an opinion and move on. Our thirst for knowledge is constant, so we prefer to listen to someone educating us on something we don't know than having to waste time sharing what we know to others. That rarely benefits us, unless we're looking for feedback.

These are precisely the skills required these days, where speed is key and time is the most precious resource we'll ever spend. But we haven't got it exactly right yet, so we keep pushing, keep on looking for that extra ingredient to add to the mix and make the perfect recipe. 'Why?' they ask us. 'Because,' we say, 'you never know...' We're not pulling up the roots every five minutes to see if the plant has grown. We prefer to explore the whole garden.

"Forever searching" by Julius! is licensed under CC BY 2.0

CARPE DIEM

We are JOATS. We have a lot of things going on, competing for our attention. Every day that we breathe a myriad of thoughts flash through our heads. Some of them stay a while, some of them we banish. Some of them are pure gold and we want to hold onto them, kick them around and develop them, but then the next thought or an interruption comes along and they're gone, sometimes forever.

You must seize the moment. You have these great thoughts milling around and you need to harness them so that you can filter them later and act on the good ones. That germ of a great one-liner. That question you must ask someone. That errand you must get done by Friday. That idea for a great new band, book, business...

Don't let these thoughts disappear into the ether!

If you're at your computer, keep a window open that you can toggle to, punch in a bullet point, and go back to what you were doing. As I write this book, every single page fires a few synapses that lead to thoughts that don't belong on there. They do belong somewhere else, maybe in the book, maybe in another area of my life, but they're important, so I stop momentarily, add them to a list and come back to where I was.

If you're out and about, or relaxing in front of something, or going from a to b, you don't need to worry about a notebook or pen to capture that gem for posterity. Learn how to use the audio memo facility on your phone, or leave yourself a voicemail.

general in life

I found myself on a plane back from the US, where I had been teaching tennis at a kids' camp for the second successive summer. I was starting my first proper job. The job was in business, which I didn't know anything about, since I had never studied it at school or college. The job was also in Liverpool, which I had been to once before for the interview, and didn't know anything about. The company was into life assurance and pensions, which was marginally more interesting than general insurance – property, cars and stuff – but it was still the kind of company that attracted actuaries because they found accountancy too interesting.

My father, quite rightly, had encouraged me to look for a job in business. You see, financial deregulation in the City of London had happened with the 'big bang' the year before, and it seemed like a good industry to get into. My father neglected to mention that his first job after National Service was as a management trainee in a factory, where he lasted eight months before embarking on a life-long career as a French and Italian teacher, finishing up as head of 'sixth form', who were the sixteen-to-eighteen-year-olds doing their last two years before departing for the world of work or further education.

The company had four strands to their graduate intake: sales, IT, actuarial and management. Not surprisingly, despite being told in the past that I have the personality for sales, I was joining the management development programme, because it was the most general and needed a broader range of skills. I didn't need to be an expert technical person, I didn't need to know the products inside out, and I didn't need to be able to calculate a mortality table. I needed to be organised, good with people and a decent communicator. A little bit of everything, and not too deep in anything. Perfect.

"Monochrome Liver Building Liverpool #dailyshoot" by Les Haines is licensed under CC BY 2.0

Ein Multitalent kann Vieles, aber nichts richtig

("A multi-talent can do much, but nothing properly")

German

"Curious. As I was folding my shirts I noticed I had similar colors to the German flag :P - alles ist gut mit die Welt" by dreammjpr is licensed under CC BY 2.0

DO NOTHING

When you're selling something to a company, the two most likely competitors you face are the two you might not be expecting. The first is an internal solution where the company reckons they can solve the problem themselves and money doesn't have to exit the building into your hands. The second is unaffectionately known as Do Nothing Inc, or 'DNI'. Here the company decides that it's doing alright, it doesn't have to invest in a change, it can afford to preserve the status quo.

When you decide to spend time reading something, it's usually because you're looking for relaxation time, or you want to acquire knowledge, or you feel you need to make a change. Setting aside the content that's designed to provide an escape from our daily lives or build our knowledge, isn't everything else trying to get you to shift your position? That's why we read a self-help book, isn't it? Either we want to figure out if we need to make a change, or we want to learn how to make a change.

As such this book is an anti-self-help book. Call it a self-acknowledgement book. If you've come to a realisation that you are indeed a JOAT, or if these words have reinforced what you knew all along, and you are happy in your 'joatness', then do nothing. By which I mean do nothing different. Keep doing what you're doing, keep building on who you are and how you approach work and life, because you're doing fine.

It feels good, doesn't it? You can approach things with a new freshness, a new vigour. It's time to make a plan.

WHY ARE THERE NO CELEBRATED JOATS?

How many well-known JOATs can you name? How many JOAT role models are there? The people in the public eye are those who are famous for one thing, not a bunch of things. They hack into government networks, they invent new devices for consuming music, they present natural history programs on TV.

"But wait," I hear you say, "what about all those famous generalists out there? Aren't CEOs and captains of industry generalists by their very nature?" While it's true that a generalist skill-set is needed to run a business, the person at the top of the company ladder didn't make the top rung by being a JOAT. They moved from one specialty to another, gathering success and experience on the way.

While the democratising power of the Internet makes it easier for more people than ever before to have a fair crack at the whip of becoming celebrated, much of what we read and hear plays the numbers game, because the lowest common denominator attracts the most attention, the highest audience, the biggest ratings, and the most money. This is why those responsible for our media go for the famous, the popular, the sensational, the disastrous. And this is the domain of those known for one thing, and not much else.

JOATs don't make for good television. It's the antithesis of everything television stands for. Maybe it doesn't make for a good book either, unless it explains, gives meaning, and provides direction. And don't confuse the JOAT with the people you see on the impossibly large range of 'reality television' programs. They're not JOATS, they're striving to be celebrated.

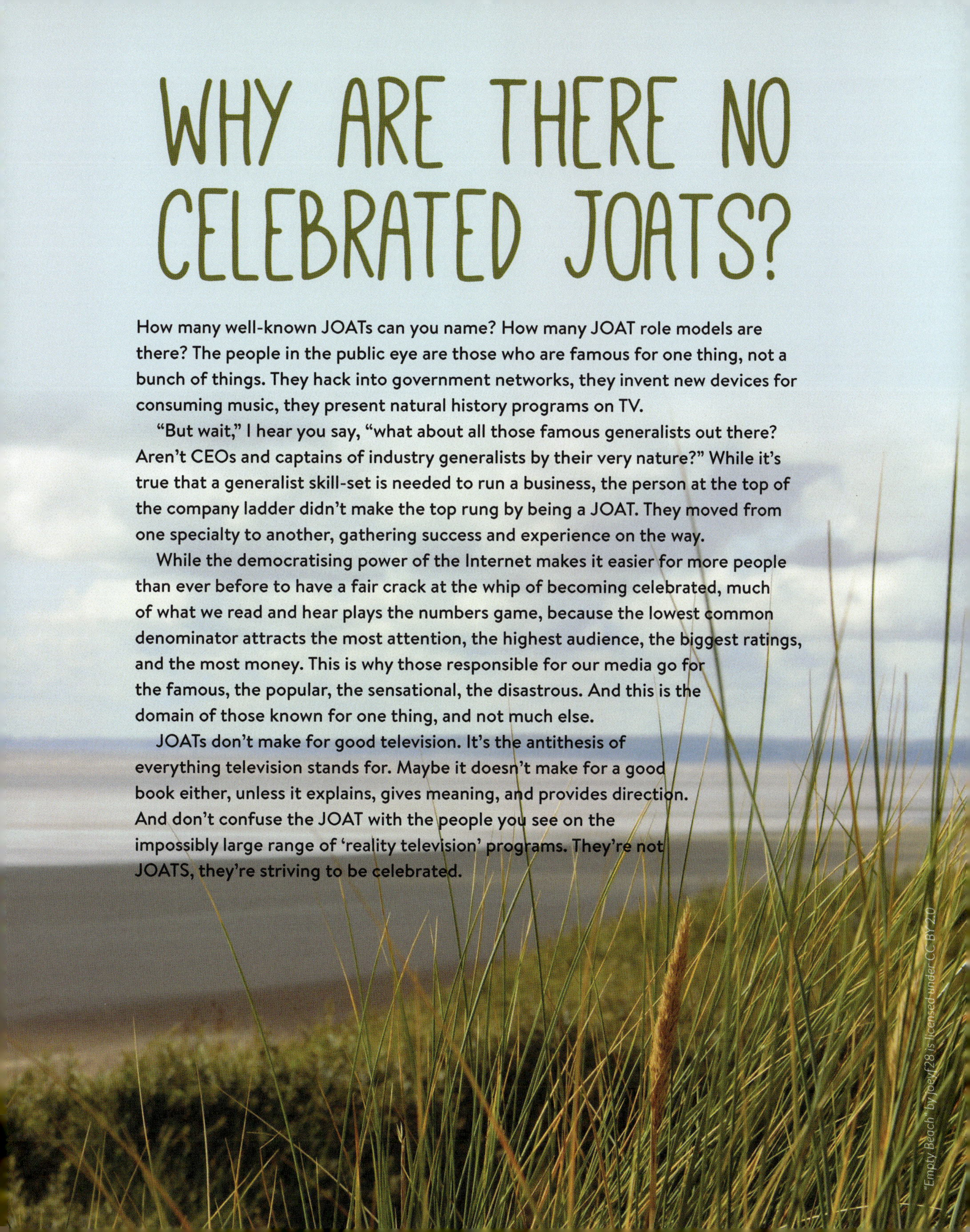

MIX NOT MESS

The word 'melange' is a lovely-sounding word. It can mean mix, in a good way. More generally though it means mess or confusion. This is the bad way. As JOATs we need to make sure that the bundle of things we do well are a good mix, not a fuddled mess. There are a few things you can do to get this right:

- Be honest in your assessment of what your skills are and how good you are at them
- Be strong in your weeding out of skills that don't make the grade, either to make room for new ones or to concentrate on elevating the qualities of one lesser skill
- Be clear in what your unique combination of skills does for people. Why should they care? How will they benefit?
- Be open to feedback from people whose opinion you trust so that you can improve both what you bring to the party and how you articulate that value to others
- Be prepared to fine-tune your skills and how you combine them, constantly
- Be attentive, because things change all the time and you have the diversity and adaptability to capitalise before the others do
- Be happy, knowing that the generalist's time has come, even though the specialist-dominated world of media and communications hasn't acknowledged it yet

Your mix is like your finger print. It's unique to you. But unlike your finger print, you're in control of it and you can mould it into something special.

"JellyBabies 0408 5511" by Ross Elliott is licensed under CC BY 2.0

master of bloody anything

After college I didn't really know what I wanted to do. So, I hedged my bets – inevitably. In addition to offers from insurance and the UK Treasury department, I also applied to do an MBA, a Master's Degree in Business Administration. They were very much in vogue in the US in the late 1980s, and just starting to become established in Europe. I got an offer with a scholarship from the University of Cincinnati's College of Business. It wasn't a prestigious top ten business school, but it had money and an openness to growing its base of international students.

Why did I think of doing an MBA? Human, emotional reasons. I had dated a US girl in my final year of college, and it had gotten serious. I wanted to prolong the relationship, she was starting an MBA in Texas – more than a thousand miles from 'Cincy' – and it seemed like a good idea. I postponed the offer from Cincy for two years, the first year while we tried to make a distance relationship work and the second year while I got an extra year of work under my belt and plucked up the courage to come over, even though by that time we had agreed the relationship had run its course.

The MBA is a generalist's dream. You get to do subjects in finance, accounting, marketing, IT, operations and international business. Then you get to specialise to an extent, all the while accruing credits and grades towards your final GPA – grade point average. I also got to do my summer internship back at the life assurance company between the two years, which got me home for three months. I wasn't a natural at business, but I worked hard – and took a job in the college office to help pay off the modest loan I had taken – and found that marketing and international was my thing.

Πολυτεχνίτης και ερημοσπίτης

("A man of many crafts and a deserted home").

Greek

"The empty house." by Elevationmann is licensed under CC BY 2.0

modern creatures

Up until quite recently, and even now in some parts of the world, we had to be specialists to get by. We were warriors, or we were hunters, or we tilled the land. Alternatively, we looked after the children, we maintained the home and made it a safe environment to bring up families.

Perhaps we were craftsmen and women, stone masons, or working in metal, wood or paint. We could have been legislators, enforcers, thinkers, philosophers. We could have tended the sick. Or we could have operated on the fringes of society as beggars, thieves, looters and con-artists.

The JOAT is a product of a modern, civilised society. We would have died in battle at the hands of a better fighter. Our paintings wouldn't have sold because there were better painters. Our land wouldn't have generated as many crops as those of the better farmers. We're better than some, but there are always too many that are faster, higher and stronger.

When you experience the dystopian extremes of creations like Brave New World, Logan's Run and the more modern crop of works like The Hunger Games and Divergent/Insurgent/Allegiant, you get a glimpse of the forced segregation, specialism and accelerated survival of the fittest associated with the breakdown of democracy and freedom.

Most of us who live in stable, free-thinking societies are modern creatures, and lucky creatures, because otherwise we JOATs would struggle to flourish. It is a modern, sophisticated but above all stable environment that allows us to embrace variety and indulge our passions in a way that allows us to put food on the table, bring up our kids safely and contribute meaningfully to society.

narrow it down

Sometimes, as a JOAT, you need to check you're OK. We all have moments of self-doubt where we need to gauge where we are on the success meter and assure ourselves that we're progressing in the direction and at the speed we want. This is a natural part of the process of making sure that life isn't passing us by.

You may feel that you're a small cog in a big machine and that your contribution is minimal at worst and could be better. Congratulations! Acknowledging this is half the battle. Commiserations! This is the easy half, but you're moving forwards. Let's assume you decide that you do need to change something for the better, that you're not happy to acquiesce in the status quo.

You need to improve your lot in life from your current lot. To do that, you need to show your current lot in your best possible light. This is mainly for yourself, so you can see the way ahead. If you narrow it down enough, you'll find that you are among the best at what you do. You work in an assembly line for medical devices? For that particular device, in that industry, you are among an elite few that can assemble the device to that level of quality. You can do each of the key jobs along that line. Someone would need a lot of training and dedication to get to your level.

You're in customer service in a call centre? In your industry, and for the products your company provides, no one knows your customers as well as you. Your generalist background means that there are few people in the world, if any, that can help with the range of specific customer queries that you can.

Narrow it down to big yourself up.

Film stars, sports stars, music stars, entrepreneurial stars, company stars, political stars. We see them in action, and for more than a moment we want to be like them. No, we want to be them. We want the trappings that come with their status and success. We get star-struck, a little overwhelmed by them if we're lucky enough to meet them or see them in person. They seem to have a presence that transcends that of mere mortals. They ooze charisma, it seems to drip out of every pore, intoxicating those around them like a pheromone.

It's easy to get a little fazed by these people. After all, we've done a fair bit of what they do. We've played tennis or football for a few years, we've done some drama, we've written songs, poems and stories. We ran for student council at school, we've managed a team of people. They're doing the same things as we are, only much better, and on a far bigger stage.

STAR-STRUCK

Except that they're not. You may think they are, but they're not. These people are playing the same sport or doing the same job as you in name only. They're not even at a different level, they're playing a different game. It's almost like they're in a different dimension, impossibly fast, controlled, assured.

Two things here: first, I'm not talking about people a few rungs higher on the ladder than you. You can reach their level and surpass them, of course you can. I'm talking about the superstar performers, the ones breathing in the rarified air. Second, I'm not saying you should give up on your dreams and settle at where you are. You have to commit yourself to the cause, and nothing else, for as long as it takes. Do you want to do that? As the late British entertainer Roy Castle – himself no lacking in ability across a trade or two – used to sing on the UK television program Record Breakers: "If you want to be the best, if you want to beat the rest, dedication's what you need."

free agency

As soon as I returned from my MBA in the US, at the beginning of 1992, I had interviews to be the marketing manager of a design and marketing agency in Edinburgh. It was a family business, I had met the son of the owner during a tennis summer in the US and we had stayed in touch. I wasn't quite a shoo-in, because there a were a few interview rounds and 80 applicants, but it certainly helped to know the people.

The great thing about working for a small company is that by its nature you're a generalist, doing a range of different things. I was hired to rebrand the company, but after that I did business development, sales, account management and a little bit of people management. I was a 'suit', not a creative, in that sense. Agencies of this size might also contract out more specialist work like copywriting, but I had a bit of a flair for it, I liked it and it suited the company's margins to keep this work in-house. It suited me fine too, and we won two awards in the process.

I worked on so-called short copy, which as the name suggests is straplines, slogans and catch phrases, that kind of thing. I also got to work on long copy, more narrative-based content for brochures and reports. As the account manager I would also take the brief from the client and contribute to the creative brainstorming process with the designers, to add my two pennies' worth and also to make sure that we stayed on track with the project.

The small business gives you freedom to develop your generalist skills.

תפסת מרובה לא תפסת - תפסת מועט תפסת

("He who has seized a lot, has not seized – He who has seized little, seized")

Hebrew

"Hebrew Letters Clock - Poster Edges Effect" by zeevveez is licensed under CC BY 2.0

10k

TEN THOUSAND HOURS

A few ground-breaking experiments have discovered that the magic formula for getting to the top of the tree in something is ten thousand hours of practice. This work was brought to the public consciousness by Malcom Gladwell in his book Outliers, and leaned on heavily by social scientists and writers everywhere, including Matthew Syed in his rather good book 'Bounce'.

This presents somewhat of a problem for the JOAT. Devoting a monopoly of our available time to one thing is not something that comes naturally to us. It's not something that we want to do either. When we're young, we like the variety of lots of different things to occupy us. We also derive a bit of comfort from the fact that we're spreading our bets. As a consequence, we don't spend enough time on the one thing that will result in the rapid, stellar improvements that jettison us into the top tier.

When we're older, there's perhaps not enough sand in the hour glass left for us to devote our ten thousand hours – or ten years at twenty hours a week – to that one thing, starting from our late departure time. There are a few things, of course, that we can excel at when we're into our lifespan's back nine holes, such as writing – provided we have most of our mental faculties and some of our physical ones. The 'Ten K' formula amplifies the truth that we JOATs have not set out our stall to be in the 1%. This is our choice. We like balance. The spoils of greatness might be nice, but we're not going to devote the majority of our free time to that end. We're all about the journey, and to hell with the destination.

NOW AND NEW

If you feel you need to make a change, to try something else, what should you do?

You should do something now. Right now has never been a better time for the JOAT. You can do a bunch of things and still make your family, your life and your finances work. It always takes longer than you think to do something, so the sooner you start, the sooner you'll get there. Do you know a single person who didn't wish – once they'd embarked on something – that they had started sooner?

OK, so it's easier said than done, which is why so many books fail to give the reader the impetus they need to get off the armchair and onto the phone or out into the world.

The secret is to forge something new. If it's new to you, great. If it's new to others, even better. If it's new to a lot of people, better again.

You are a JOAT, so forge a new job or a new business that lies at the intersection of the things that you do pretty well.

Find companies that need people fitting your skills combination. If they don't have vacancies in those roles, or those roles don't exist, can you make a case for them creating a role for you? Can you demonstrate the answer to the question they're all thinking: can we make money or garner kudos from this person?

Start something that combines the things you enjoy doing, the things you do well and the things you conclude people will pay for. Is someone already doing that? Great, it means money can be made there. How can your unique combination deliver better customer satisfaction than they currently deliver?

make two lists

Make two lists. In one list put all the things you're good at. In the other list put all the things you like doing. Take as long – or as little – as you like.

Have a look at the two lists. How long is your 'good' list? How long is your 'like' list? Which things are on both your lists? Which are on one list but not the other?

Very few people make the distinction between like and good. The most common refrain you'll hear is this: "I don't like it, I'm no good at it." This acknowledges there is a causal relationship between the two, but it's unclear what the direction of causality is.

The relationship is clearer when it's in the positive. "I like this wine, therefore, as far as I'm concerned, this is a good wine." "I like biology, I'm good at it." There is a difference between the two, but you will occasionally hear the occasional comment from a thoughtful person. "It's a good film, but I didn't like it." "I like playing football. Am I good at football, no." "I don't enjoy managing people, but I know that I do it well."

If you're looking for something new, you first need to concentrate your efforts on a combination of items in your good list. Then you need to see which of them are things you like as well.

Liking something gives you the energy and drive you need to push through to something new. People care about what you're good at, because that makes the difference for them. They will pay you attention and money for what makes a difference. Why should they care what you like doing? It makes no difference to them, and all the difference to you.

LIFE
LIST
JOURNAL
BIC

the sporting all-rounder

Even within the confines of a single sport, I became an all-rounder. I had a fair amount of skill in rugby, but with its emphasis on size and speed I was soon swallowed up. I started out as scrum half, because I was tiny, but as the rest of the world grew, and I didn't, I was moved out to the wing. At beginner and junior levels of rugby, if you're on the wing you might as well be in your back garden. The chance of three or four passes being completed before the ball gets to you was very remote.

In football, my agility and skill level meant I could play pretty much anywhere, but my lack of size meant that I was not a lumbering defender nor a centre forward. I therefore settled in wing and midfield positions. In cricket, I started out as a bowler, but I wasn't the quickest in the team so I generally came on after the first bowling change. As I got older, I started to get the hang of batting and gradually moved up the batting order from eleven to three, four or five. I was happy to field anywhere.

These days, apart from going to the gym where I run – but not too far to be a runner – and do weights – but not so heavy as to become a gym monkey, I play five-a-side soccer on artificial pitches. It's a different game from the grassy eleven-a-side version. I practice playing in different positions to improve my all-around game. I'm the oldest there, so I start in goal and then ease myself further into the game by playing defense, then midfield and finally attack.

Aki sokat markol, keveset fog

("He who grasps much, retains but little")

Hungarian

THE JOAT DIET

As long as we've had the luxury of being able to pick and choose between foods, we've had decisions to make. Whether we view it as a pleasure, a necessity, a means to an end, or somewhere in between, we've been obsessed with what we eat.

Diet crazes come and go. Foods have fallen in and out of favour. Supplements are good for you, supplements are bad for you. And so on.

Throughout all of this, one diet has always been there, and always will be. The balanced diet is the true lasting diet. It's not difficult to see why. Balance is good. It restores our equilibrium.

If we're athletes we need a different kind of diet. If we're underweight or overweight we need a different kind of diet. If we have certain illnesses, conditions or allergies, we need a different kind of diet. Many of these diets are temporary, while we excel physically at our highest level or fix a particular problem. Once that period is over, or once we get to where we need to be physically and mentally, then it's a balanced diet that sustains us over the long term.

The central JOAT strength is founded on balance, the balance between all the things we do. Just as the balanced diet has stood the test of time in nutritional and wellbeing terms, so is the JOAT approach to life the one that gives lasting happiness and fulfilment.

purple patches

"In the zone", they call it. Those moments that feel like an out of body experience, where you're not consciously aware of doing something. It's happening by itself in a glorious harmony of timing, flow, muscle memory and mental equilibrium. They're more recognisable in sport, but of course they also happen in our working lives, where that piece of work simply comes together beautifully, we absolutely nail that presentation, or our students collectively and simultaneously have that light-bulb moment.

Purple patches don't happen that often, but when they do, it's the dual feelings of serenity and excitement – two feelings that you don't see together too often – that reward us for the thousands of hours of effort we've put into something. We try to seize the moment, hold onto it, so that we can perhaps replicate it. I've had a few of those moments – who hasn't? – in both my sporting life and working life. They are incredibly self-affirming and energising. We relive them often, perhaps embellishing them over time in our heads – which is no bad thing for our self-esteem and self-belief.

For JOATs dividing themselves between a number of skills, these purple patches represent a huge shot in the arm. They provide us with a priceless endorsement that we are good enough, perhaps as good as or better than some specialists, and we know we've got so much more to offer besides. This mental slingshot effect spurs us on both to keep improving in this area and to do as well in the other key areas that make up our work-life balance.

remember this

Don't beat yourself up.

It's not just business that craves the superlative. You see it in work and play. People expect it in their heroes of the field, stage or screen. What happened to good and better as well as best? It's no longer enough to be good or better than the rest, it's got to be superlative.

You're not giving up if you come to the realisation that you can't be the best there is out there. You're not abdicating your responsibility simply because you are not master of one thing. You're not settling for second best. You're not making up the numbers.

That's because you're running a different race. Your race. You're competing against yourself and you keep winning, you keep improving.

That's the funny thing about being in a race of one: you're the first, but you're also the last. You're the best, but also the worst. See yourself as the winner, not the loser, and keep working for victory.

general (of) marketing management

Two things happened during my agency stint in the early-to-late 1990s, one of slightly more significance to you, one of slightly more significance to me. Firstly, the Internet and world wide web happened. Second, I met my future wife at a wedding in Ireland. The first signaled a seismic shift in global business and suddenly IT was cool. The second was equally seismic to my mind and necessitated me getting myself over to Ireland as soon as I could.

I managed to combine the two by securing a job as the head of marketing for a software company that developed solutions for the insurance industry. It was looking to move from 'on premise' software to web-based – or what is now ubiquitously known as 'cloud' – technology. My marketing and insurance experience served me well during the application process, but I knew next to nothing about IT, except that it was the future. The company decided I was worth the risk and so I started work in Dublin towards the end of 1997.

This was my first exposure to marketing management, with a team of specialists under me. We had people responsible for generating demand, inside sales people who would qualify customers on the phone and try and make appointments for the field sales people, and website people who designed, implemented and managed the ever-evolving websites. I looked after corporate marketing and the brand. Fortunately for me, I had some degree of experience in all these areas, and so I was able to manage them while learning about the software industry. I had made the transition to an exciting industry that still to a large extent pays the bills.

"Union General George S. Greene -- Culp's Hill Gettysburg (PA) National Military Park 2012" by Ron Cogswell is licensed under CC BY 2.0

Esperto di tutto, maestro in niente

("Expert of everything, master of none")

Italian

"Maestro Nobile Vol. 7 -1942-1949- Herbert Von Karajan Documents" by iClassicalCom is licensed under CC BY 2.0

THE JOAT LONG TAIL

There is a phenomenon in business when you look at something like a sales or distribution curve. It's called the 'long tail'. Along the horizontal 'x' axis are the different things or products. Along the vertical 'y' axis are the various amounts of the products, their popularity if you like. If you arrange then with the most popular or most-selling things on the left, down to the least popular or fewest-selling items on the right, you get a curve with a pretty standard shape.

The left-hand side of the curve is the high part, known as the head, where all the popular products are. The head then tapers off down to the right until the curve is barely above the x axis. This tapering part is known as the long tail, and if you have a very large list of products, then you have a very long tail. When you think about traditional retail outlets and broadcasting channels, for example, all you can ever get is the head, the most popular items. The outlets don't have the space to stock anything other than the few hundred most popular things, and the broadcasters don't have time to mention the smaller items, nor could they afford to if they wanted to bolster their ratings.

The Internet has made it possible for people and companies to make money by servicing the long tail, and catering to a global audience with an almost infinite number of ultra-niche requirements, as long as the audience can find you, especially if the cost of replicating and distributing those products is close to zero, as in digital goods.

More importantly, for the JOAT lurking down in the long tail, it makes it possible for you to find and satisfy the requirements of people who need precisely your unique combination of abilities.

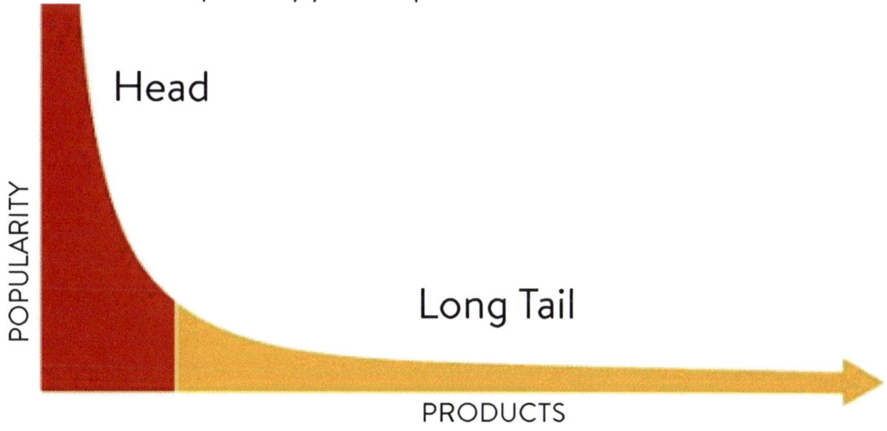

the path is

OK, so you're absorbing some of this content and you accept that you are a JOAT, but you don't want to be one any more. You want to aim highest, become a specialist, and get to the top of your chosen tree. It's a perfectly noble goal to set yourself. You see, we JOATs are very good at sliding into the next new experience and acquiring another arrow for our quiver. It's what we've always done. But, leaving generalism behind and taking the first tentative steps on the path towards true mastery is a different kettle of fish.

In one of my previous jobs, whenever I felt like I was stuck in the weeds for a few weeks and needed someone else's perspective, I used to go to my mentor for a chat. He was a brilliant individual, a successful businessman and a genuine visionary. He would listen to my situation, put it to one side and then draw on a whiteboard his vision of where the company would be in two years, how it would capitalise on market forces, that kind of thing.

I used to come away from these sessions with feelings of elation and despondency in equal measure. Elated that the future of the company was in safe hands and that the future was bright. Despondent that I was still stuck where I was and still didn't know how I could get to the promised land. The path to specialism is rarely clear for us JOATs. To key to starting on that path is to start. Taking baby steps and biting off small digestible chunks – to mix metaphors – allow you to reach some mini-milestones and at the same time review your journey so far and check you're on the right course.

rarely clear

simple over complex

You might think that the JOAT likes things to be as intertwined and complicated as possible, a mass of tangled thoughts and activities to match their busy, even hectic approach to life and work. "Yes, I have so much going on, I can barely keep track of it all." This is not the case; in fact, the opposite is true.

To maintain the variety and breadth, the JOAT takes the high-level approach to things, searching out the essence of each of them, which makes it easier to compartmentalise the knowledge and easier to make good decisions. Too much information, and it starts to crowd out the other aspects of the JOAT's life, or else gets lost in a fog of surfeit.

For this reason the JOAT craves simplicity over complexity. It serves the JOAT well when they are transferring information, imparting knowledge, or briefing a supplier. "If I could distil all this information down into one key message for you ... if you take away one thing from this session, it would be ..." This is why when someone's pitching a new idea at you, it helps you picture and remember it when they say "It's like an iPhone on steroids", "It's Twitter for Tots", "the Chinese Facebook", or "The Taking of Pelham 123 Meets Speed".

The JOAT strives to make it easy for their audience, reasoning that if it's too hard, or too confusing, or too difficult, it won't get done and change for the better won't happen. So, you see, some of the JOAT's best traits are the ingredients of successful working and living: communicating clearly with people and being thoughtful and easy to get on with.

the consulting-contracting angles

The late 1990s dot com boom that contributed to my rise through the software ranks to a posting in Richmond, Virginia in the US also dealt the hammer blow of redundancy later that year - 2001 - when boom went to bust. Cast adrift with a four-week-old baby in tow, we returned to Ireland to my in-laws to lick our wounds. The timing couldn't have been better, as it gave me a few months off to add a new skill to my portfolio, namely full-time new Dad.

Ireland's IT industry was stumbling badly in early 2002 and so we headed across to England to find work. I was offered a role of Commercial Director with a small company in the document management systems business that wanted to get into secure email solutions. I like working for small companies, but this was very small, a two-year start-up and so they wanted me to be a contractor rather than an employee. I needed the job, so took it, but this also led to me starting a marketing consultancy that continues to this day. The lines between consultant and contractor blur somewhat, but in my view if you're a contractor you're told what to do and if you're a consultant you get to advise what to do, and then do it.

Yet again I had managed by serendipity to add new strings to my bow: the consulting/contracting side, still in sales and marketing, and the commercial side, with responsibility across both sales and marketing. This 'twin track' approach of consulting and employment gives me options and allows me to slot in project-based work while I keep an eye on career roles in case I want to go back to life in Employee City.

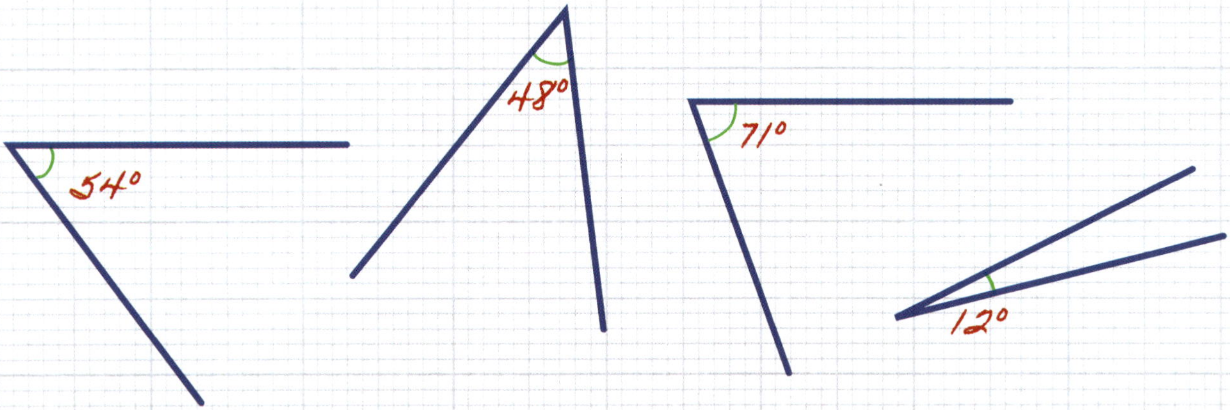

多芸は無芸

("Many talents is no talent")

Japanese

THE JOAT-MASTER SPECTRUM

JOAT, or master of one? It's a question of degree, a case of where you sit on the JOAT-Master spectrum. Almost all of us specialise to a certain extent, but not an extent enough to make it our speciality. And almost all of us are, to a degree, JOATs. That's the paradox that many of us struggle with on a daily basis.

If you work in a software company, you might be a software developer, someone who writes code. Maybe you're a master at one type of programming language, but more likely you're good at a few of them. You're unlikely to be the person left to your own devices for years while you invent something completely new and big like Java.

If you also work in that same software company, you might work

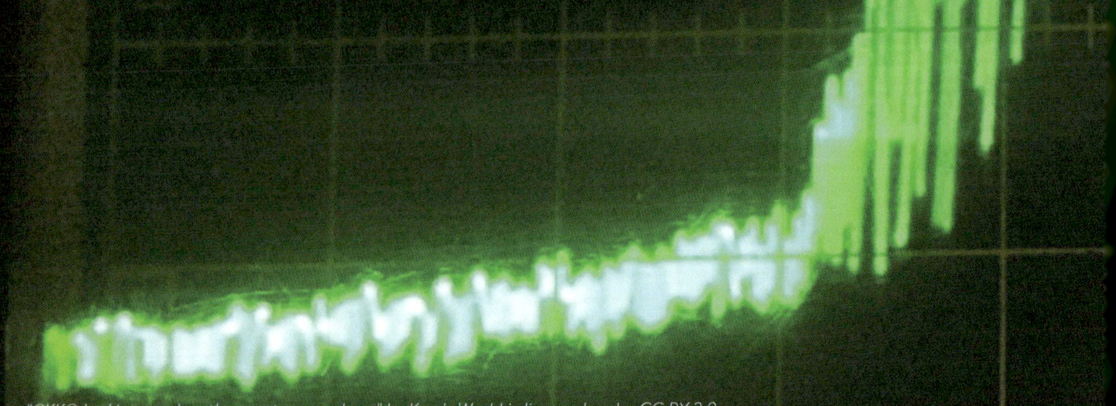

"CKKQ looking good on the spectrum analyzer" by Kam's World is licensed under CC BY 2.0

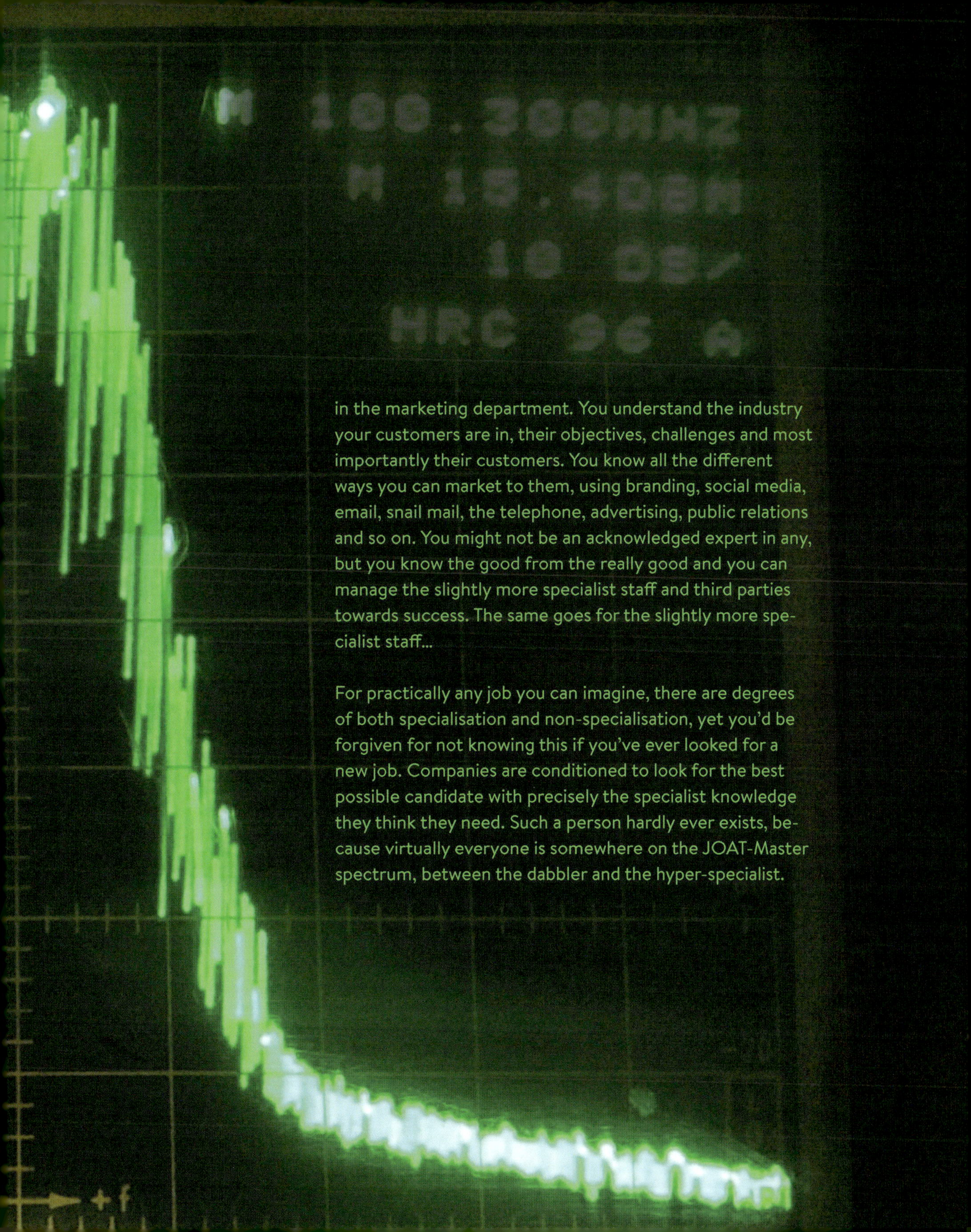

in the marketing department. You understand the industry your customers are in, their objectives, challenges and most importantly their customers. You know all the different ways you can market to them, using branding, social media, email, snail mail, the telephone, advertising, public relations and so on. You might not be an acknowledged expert in any, but you know the good from the really good and you can manage the slightly more specialist staff and third parties towards success. The same goes for the slightly more specialist staff...

For practically any job you can imagine, there are degrees of both specialisation and non-specialisation, yet you'd be forgiven for not knowing this if you've ever looked for a new job. Companies are conditioned to look for the best possible candidate with precisely the specialist knowledge they think they need. Such a person hardly ever exists, because virtually everyone is somewhere on the JOAT-Master spectrum, between the dabbler and the hyper-specialist.

the power of research

We JOATs can sometimes find ourselves naturally drifting from one opportunity to the next, and when we look back on each step we took in life, we often justify the step by saying 'well, that may not have turned out as I expected it to, but I learned this and it allowed me to do that.' It's perfectly OK to argue that every decision was a good decision in retrospect, as long as we quickly click back to the present and where we want to go from here.

There are times, though, when that next natural opportunity doesn't come to us when we need it. Then we have to go looking for it, and make it ours.

When was the last time you saw a job ad for someone with the words Jack of All Trades or even generalist in it? Job ads are written by specialists – or under the instruction of specialists – who want specialists because that's who they think they need for the role. "Get me the very best accountant you can. They need to be insanely great and have ten years' experience in exactly our line of work, using all the systems we use." Ok...

You need to get lucky, and you get lucky with effort. Do the research on the kinds of organisations who might not even know they need your combination of skills – yet. Do the research on your personal network of contacts. You get jobs sometimes because of whom you know, and when you're a JOAT you need that extra leg up, that extra endorsement from the inside. "I know someone who'd be perfect for you" is unbelievably powerful coming from a trusted person.

the best mixers are JOATs

We JOATs are the best mixers. It's the default generalist behaviour. Think about it.

If we're a JOAT, the chances are that one of those trades is our interpersonal skills. Because we're always on the lookout for some new trade to add to our skillset, we're attentive and we listen well. We notice body language and social queues. Because we've tried a few things we find it easier to relate to other people. We've more chance of having something in common with them.

The good mixer is probably not a shy introvert who prefers their own company and would rather be doing their own thing. We have to work hard with introverts to get them to come out of their shell and feel comfortable engaging with us. The good mixer is probably not a brash extrovert who works hard to be the centre of attention. We tend to avoid these people socially because they dominate the conversation and there's not a fair exchange in the dialogue process.

The JOAT does not have the star quality to stop a room dead when they enter. We're not the unnoticed person lurking in the corner. We're somewhere in the middle, easy to talk to, and interested in what others have to say. We can listen properly, and we can offer a constructive opinion. We are generous with our attention. This is because, secretly, we're always looking to learn from those around us.

musical non-maestro

As a person with diverse interests, I like most types of music. I don't usually write or work to music, and I'm not usually the first to put the radio on, but I do enjoy music. I think I could live without it, though, if I absolutely had to.

My one chief exposure to the world of musical instruments was a year of clarinet when I was eleven, my first year up at 'big school'. I wasn't great, I didn't enjoy it. I couldn't read music, so I wrote the letters of each note under the songs and brought the book into my lesson, only for my instructor to erase them all.

I still can't read music. The only think I do musically is what most JOATs do. I can sing a bit. I sang in the choir at school. At university, a friend of mine who is genuinely musical thought I could hold a note, and thus was born an on-off affair in amateur recording of euro-pop songs. I've been in a proper recording studio, and I know how to record a song, but I wouldn't rate myself as a master singer, not by a long chalk.

My friend and I still record the occasional euro-pop ditty, 30 years on. He does everything – literally everything – including the guide vocal. I turn up, we do the vocal a few times, 'punch in' the bits I didn't get right, and then we're done. I tell myself that if he ever submitted the work to get a recording contract or to attract the attention of someone of influence, my voice is good enough to give them the idea of its potential, and not much more.

Careers in the pop world have been founded on less ability, I know, but for me music is barely enough of a skill to keep in the basket of my current trades.

열 두 가지 재주 가진 놈이 저녁거리가 없다

("A man of twelve talents has nothing to eat for dinner")

Korean

"Empty cupboard" by rubyblossom. is licensed under CC BY-SA 2.0

THE NEVER-ENDING CAREER

As I write this page I am fifty years and eleven months of age. This is significant to me because it was the precise age at which my Dad retired from his full-time teaching job after a life-time in education. My Mum followed later when she was 55. A number of things played to their advantage for retiring so early, but the main factor was that in the early 1980s the 'baby boomer' population had peaked. School rolls were starting to fall and the government was encouraging teachers to go early on a full pension. Nice. Unusually for that generation, my folks had loads of things to keep body and mind active and they enjoyed more than two decades of an active lifestyle together. Not for them the withering on the vine and the premature death once full-time work ceases. That's not what you pay into a pension for.

For my generation, the prospect of retirement before seventy years and eleven months of age seems a remote possibility. An ageing population, a major financial downturn and being older than the average parental age have conspired to put us in hock to the filthy lucre for a good while to come, until we get ourselves, and our kids, financially independent.

This is fortunate for the JOAT, because a portfolio career provides the perfect balance for extending ourselves well past retirement age. As masters of our own destiny we can move the different levers up or down depending on our financial needs, our energy levels and our free time requirements. We have the flexibility and we have the control. This is harder to do if we are specialists or hold down one full-time occupation.

FAMOUS JOATS

1.

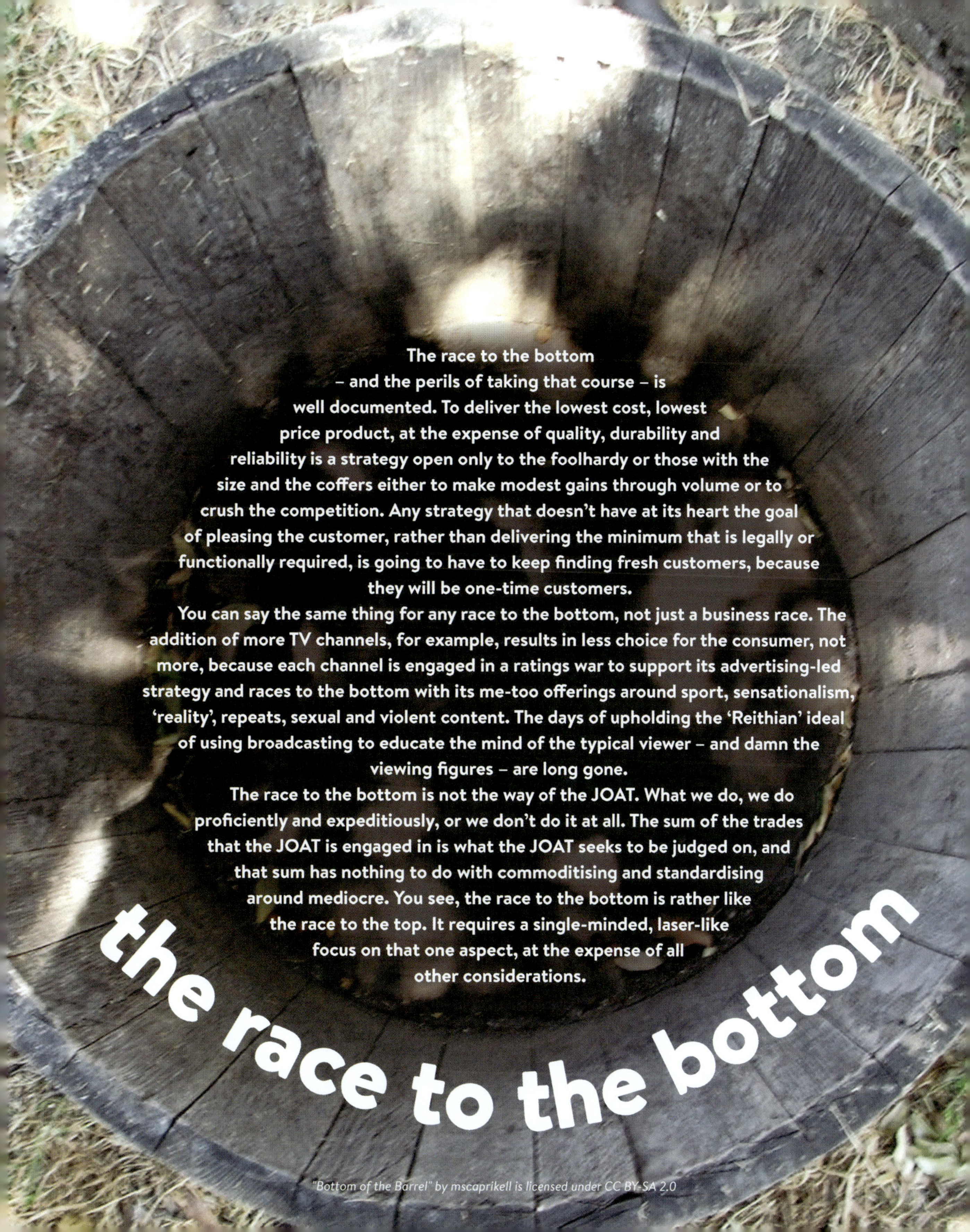

the race to the bottom

The race to the bottom – and the perils of taking that course – is well documented. To deliver the lowest cost, lowest price product, at the expense of quality, durability and reliability is a strategy open only to the foolhardy or those with the size and the coffers either to make modest gains through volume or to crush the competition. Any strategy that doesn't have at its heart the goal of pleasing the customer, rather than delivering the minimum that is legally or functionally required, is going to have to keep finding fresh customers, because they will be one-time customers.

You can say the same thing for any race to the bottom, not just a business race. The addition of more TV channels, for example, results in less choice for the consumer, not more, because each channel is engaged in a ratings war to support its advertising-led strategy and races to the bottom with its me-too offerings around sport, sensationalism, 'reality', repeats, sexual and violent content. The days of upholding the 'Reithian' ideal of using broadcasting to educate the mind of the typical viewer – and damn the viewing figures – are long gone.

The race to the bottom is not the way of the JOAT. What we do, we do proficiently and expeditiously, or we don't do it at all. The sum of the trades that the JOAT is engaged in is what the JOAT seeks to be judged on, and that sum has nothing to do with commoditising and standardising around mediocre. You see, the race to the bottom is rather like the race to the top. It requires a single-minded, laser-like focus on that one aspect, at the expense of all other considerations.

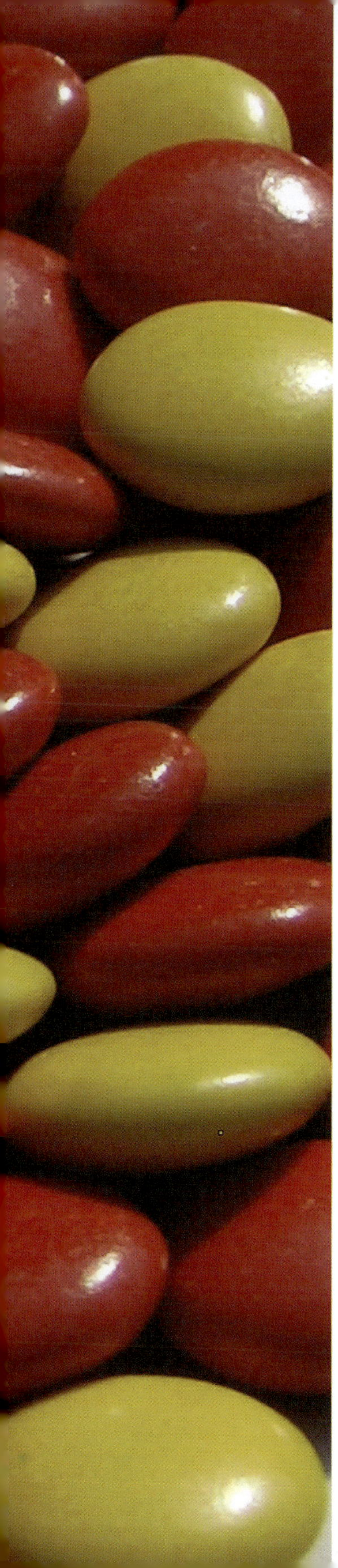

the happy hybrid

My contracting work was never going to last indefinitely, so towards the end of 2003 I moved to a great role looking after the email branding service of a high-flying managed IT security services provider. The branding service was the poor relation of the other security services, and was a political hot potato. I was keen to make it work, so I did everything to make it a success: the selling, the implementation, the partner management, even the technical support. This, of course, played to my generalist strengths as well.

In the end, though, the service was doomed to be 'sunsetted', but I had done enough to impress the powers that be to allow me to move into a role that was half demand generation for Europe, and half product marketing for the worldwide operation. Once more I had the chance to spread my expertise across more than one area and divided my time fifty-fifty. I got the chance to visit the key markets and work closely with the people and agencies on the ground. It also gave me the platform to move into a more specialist role – yes, it's true – doing full-time product marketing for the company's range of email and web security services.

Within the same company and within the space of two years I had managed to move from selling a marketing service to marketing a security service, via a hybrid role that combined two different types of marketing. Even though I eventually moved into a more specialist area of marketing I still had the broad remit that I craved, looking after a range of product lines and a number of regions.

Devyni amatai, dešimtas – badas

("When you have nine trades, then your tenth one is famine/starvation")

Lithuanian

"Famine" by Anosmia is licensed under CC BY 2.0

the race to the top

But what about the race to the top? Every business book and every 'self-help' manual extolls the virtues of setting your targets on being number 1, the chieftain. Aim for the top, they say, and the rest will follow.

The race to the top is hard. So many people want to get there, and there's only room for one, and sometimes, paradoxically not even for one. It's a constant struggle of trench warfare and healthy competitive paranoia. As part of my MBA degree in the US we played a game of running our own trainer shoe company against teams of other trainer manufacturers. Teams input their weekly strategy and a software program factored all the inputs and spat out the results in terms of market share, revenues, stock, raw supplies and so on. Ours was the only team racing to the top. Every other team chose the race to the bottom. We were marginalised by the imaginary market, and we were killed.

Is the race to the top a wise strategy for the JOAT? Can they get to the very top of any trade given their skill-set and the way they view the world? And is even entertaining this question propounding a defeatist attitude that you can't change anything, so why bother? Not at all, because this is your race, to your top. It's about being the best you can be, on your terms, upholding your ideals. It's also about understanding, when you feel a pang of human jealousy at the rise of others, that their race is not your race, and their top is not your top.

JOAT work ethic and culture

The JOAT's warm, cosy chair by the fire is variety, not speciality. It's many small things rather than one big thing. Give the JOAT an inch, and they'll take an inch, an ounce and an hour. The JOAT values many strings to the bow, not one big string, and prefers the high level on multiple topics to the detail in one topic. Breadth over depth every time.

This doesn't necessarily mean that the JOAT is a spinner of many plates, keeping lots of projects on the go at the same time. The JOAT may also pick off small chunks of digestible, doable things and perhaps finish one thing and move onto the next, taking things sequentially rather than simultaneously.

The JOAT has a strong work ethic, a speedy work rate and an almost unending enthusiasm brought on by the stimulation of the new and the different. The JOAT is sometimes not naturally disposed to certain things, and can be 'late to the party' and late to get good at something. Because we're naturally adaptable, however, we quickly catch up and overtake others because we see the applicability of what we've learned to other areas that we're familiar with.

Where does the JOAT thrive? In open, honest, collaborative environments where work is enjoyable. Because, let's face it, with work filling five days a week, and demanding five school nights a week, it had better be enjoyable, hadn't it?

speculate to accumulate

Do you know the one thing that stops most of us JOATs in our tracks, momentarily, from time to time? It's the little voice of fear.

"I don't know jack!"

"I can't do anything!"

By which you mean you can't do any one thing really well.

You think that not having a lot of depth in one area makes you vulnerable.

"I have no depth! I must get some depth! I must go deeper!"

But you overlook the fact that at this point in your life as a generalist you have accumulated a lot of experiences that make you more rounded and better able to deal with new stuff. Stuff you may have seen working in another industry, another time, or another place, that you can use to your advantage.

We can't predict the future, so we're stuck with this new stuff.

That's why we JOATs use ABS, a different kind of ABS.

Always Be Speculating. Always be looking for something new, something additional that you can accumulate for your treasure trove of things you do pretty well.

So when that little voice of fear appears on your shoulder, suggesting you can't do anything, hoping for a crisis of confidence, simply hit the ABS.

It'll fly right off, through the windscreen.

"Old slot machine" by Valerie Everett is licensed under CC BY-SA 2.0

the marketing of selling

The product marketing role I fulfilled in the UK in the mid-noughties was, for me, fairly specialised. When the company came to make itself leaner for buy-out, as a well-paid person with no direct staff I was made redundant. Or should I say, my role was made redundant. No matter, we had been planning to move back to Ireland at some point to bring up our kids there, so we simply accelerated our plans. I did some consulting work with a sister company of my previous employer, reigniting the consulting practice, while we sold our house and I kept an eye open for either employment or consulting opportunities in the Emerald Isle.

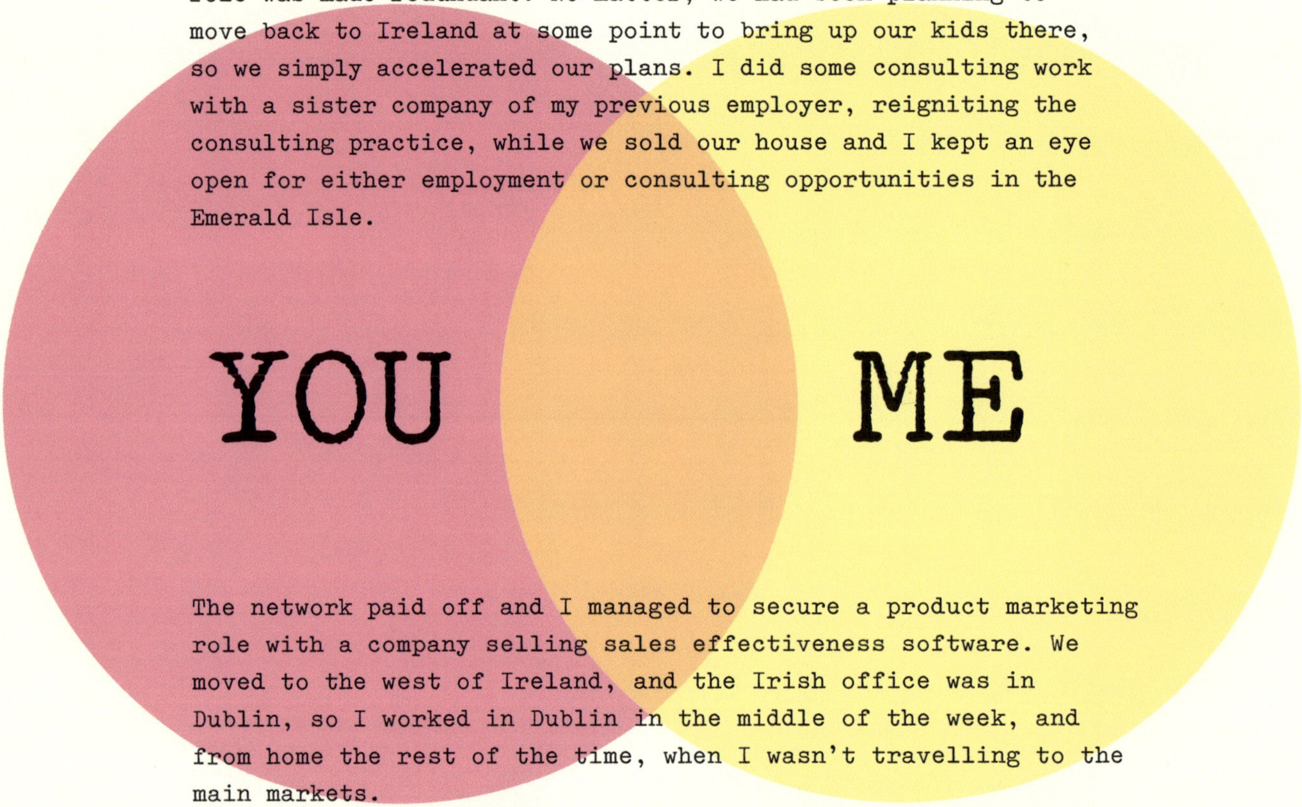

The network paid off and I managed to secure a product marketing role with a company selling sales effectiveness software. We moved to the west of Ireland, and the Irish office was in Dublin, so I worked in Dublin in the middle of the week, and from home the rest of the time, when I wasn't travelling to the main markets.

Now this might seem like a further specialisation, but when you look a little deeper, a different truth emerges. First, I was doing global product marketing but also demand generation for Europe, while also hosting and delivering webinars – a new skill for me. Second, having sold marketing services, I was now marketing a selling service and picking up some rigorous background in the art and science of how to sell properly. Third, I had a fantastic work/life balance, learning how to work from home and spend time with family part of the week, while getting office and meeting interaction for the other part.

همه کاره و هیچ کاره

("All trades and no trades")

Persian

THE LUCKY FEW

Have you ever wondered what it would be like to win the lottery? It happens to someone somewhere, most weeks of the year. Taken against the population as a whole of course, the winners represent a terribly small fraction of that population, those for whom a massive windfall has occurred, without having to do much at all. Riches beyond their wildest dreams.

What about those who live to be a hundred, or even a hundred and ten? Billions of people have graced the planet yet we only have documented evidence of an almost infinitesimally small number of people who have lived for more than a century and a decade. These are the precious few for whom DNA and happenstance have combined – or conspired, depending on your viewpoint – to give them the longest life, the greatest chance to evade mortality.

Can we say the same about the holocaust survivor? To have outlived some of the most horrific circumstances in the human story, these people must have been blessed with an abundance of luck, and perhaps saddled with an equal amount of guilt as a consequence. When we look at these people, and listen to them, do we consider them lucky, and do they describe themselves that way as well?

We are not the people whom the one in a million chance has plucked from obscurity. We are the vast majority who understand that it's OK to play the lottery and to live healthily but that we shouldn't count on luck to bring us happiness, wealth and security. What's more, these kinds of trappings don't always come to those who are the fortunate few either. We spread our bets, we seek out variety and we do our best accordingly.

REVERTING TO TYPE

People don't like change. They're uncomfortable with it, they resist it. Change is hard, and it's hard to change, so they revert to type, almost always.

Ask anyone in the training industry and if they're honest with you they'll say that it's so hard to make change stick. You're dealing with engrained behaviours.

Even we JOATs, who live for variety and multiplicity, sometimes find it hard to keep our natural adaptability going.

Here are some things you can do to keep changing, keep improving:

- Set yourself some goals for where you want to be. You know the drill: Specific, Measurable, Actionable, Realistic, Time-bound goals. For example, "I want to be able to learn use a graphics software package by the end of the quarter so that I can successfully publish my local drama club's next production being held two months later."
- Critically, identify the right behaviours for your improvement. It's the behaviours that lead to the results. For example, "by the end of the first week I will have identified and bought the best package for the job. I will then spend a minimum of one hour a day for the rest of month 1 playing with the software. I will not allow any distractions during this hour. I will learn how to do a dozen basic things on page layout." And so on...
- Monitor those behaviours. Are you doing the right things? If not, fix them, today
- Set review dates for after you've achieved your goal. Do you still want to keep this skill going? Are you still doing the right things? If not, how will you fix this?

Don't wait to see how the results turn out, or it'll be too late. You won't have changed anything.

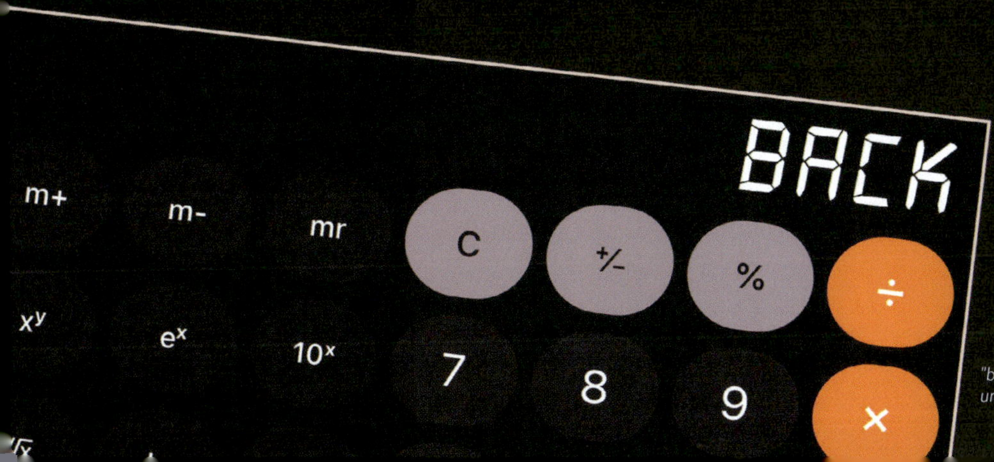

"back" by CreditDebitPro is licensed under CC BY 2.0

the grey JOAT

When my Dad was in his late sixties he said to me, "I can honestly say that my life has improved with every passing decade." I can't accurately convey to you how good that made me feel about my life, which at the time was about half way through his, and subject to the occasional thirty-something crisis that besets many of us. My Mum is now in her ninth decade. She admits that she still hasn't found what she's looking for, but while she was looking she gave back to people for over half a century, teaching children and adults in both paid and voluntary capacities. And she's still looking. She is healthy, active, busy and lives a varied, happy life.

You see, it's not the meek that will inherit the earth. The grey-haired JOATs have already beaten them to it, and not just because there's more of them and they're living longer.

Being a JOAT becomes richer and more rewarding as you get older. You've spent more time alive, you've amassed more skills, you've made more mistakes than younger folk. In short, you're a better, more finely-tuned JOAT than younger JOATs, and you're still improving.

What's more, if you've been relatively prudent and relatively fortunate in your life, you now have the disposable income to experience far more and indulge your 'joatness' to its fullest. I don't need to tell you to go out there and do it; you're probably doing it already.

Oscar Wilde once said that the young know everything, the middle aged suspect everything and the old believe everything. You can flip this when it comes to the grey JOAT.

"old people on a bus" by alainlm is licensed under CC BY 2.0

the graveyard of ambition?

After over 5 years working in the sales effectiveness business, I felt it was time for a change. Rather than have a change forced on me, outside of my control, I decided to take the initiative. I had been starting to miss out on the development of my kids, since as far as they were concerned they didn't see me after bedtime on a Monday until dinner time on a Thursday. I was also overlooked for the chief marketing role in the business a couple of times and felt I was not considered to have the required calibre - or maybe specialisation - for the role.

I secured an exciting role a short commute from my home, in charge of marketing and inside sales, and on the small management team. On paper it was a great fit for me, a cloud software small business looking for a range of experiences and skills that I had done at previous companies. I threw myself into the role, and spent the first three months building up the big three pillars any small business requires - people, processes and technology.

Unfortunately, the dream job didn't work out, and I left after eight months. We were living in a very attractive part of the country, but with a very small software industry and a place sometimes referred to as the 'graveyard of ambition'. Senior 'tech' marketing roles in this area came along with the frequency of blue moons. If I wanted the family to stay here, I would need to get creative. I dusted off the consultancy business and pursued projects with contacts in the UK and Ireland while I kept my eyes open for another great job in the locality.

Siedem fachów, ósma bieda

("Seven trades, the eighth one – poverty")
Polish

"Empty Table" by neil alejandro is licensed under CC BY 2.0

Many non-fiction books are written with the intent of helping us to do something. We read them because we're interested in the subject matter, or we want a few pointers, or we're looking to make a change in our lives. These books seek to give us the stimulus to take the initiative and break out of our current behaviour, adopt a new behaviour and keep adopting it until it becomes engrained as the 'new' current behaviour.

This is, of course, incredibly hard for us to do. It's because there have to be conditions in place for change to happen. We need to have bought into the reasons for the change, we need to see role models, we need to be guided appropriately, we need to reward the right behaviours early rather than waiting for the results to tell us it's too late, we need to celebrate the successes, and so on. How can a book possibly do all that?

This book tries to be different. It doesn't need to do anything. It tries to get you to understand three things. First, what being a JOAT really means. Second, that there are strengths in your skill-set and the way you are put together. Third, that this is a good thing, that you should be happy with this. If you can do better, go do better.

JOAT is not a taboo phrase. You're not a second-class citizen because you're not a master of one thing. You don't have to attend a self-help group to say "Hello everyone, my name is Paul and I'm a Jack of All Trades." Keep calm and carry on as you are, you're doing fine.

KEEP CALM AND CARRY ON

IF YOU ONLY READ ONE PAGE...

...READ THIS ONE

This is your time. The world is smaller. The Internet has shrunk it. The Internet, which threatened to take so many jobs away, or so people thought, has created so many more.

Large companies are on the wane. Small companies are growing in massive numbers. People are becoming consultants, contractors, sole operators, artists, starting small businesses, thriving businesses.

People in small or sole enterprises are doing their thing. But not just that, they're doing many things. In a small business you have to. There's not the scale to have specialists. Guess whose strengths that plays to? That's right, your strengths.

Specialties and specialists belong in large companies, and who wants to work for a large company anymore? Unless that large company thinks and structures itself as a group of small agile businesses, it's going to struggle, and so will you.

I found myself gravitating to small companies by mistake. I thought I belonged in a behemoth. It was my generalist skillset that was most suited to small businesses, where I achieved more, and where I found the most job happiness.

The economic and global forces are aligning themselves in favour of those who can do many things.

And here you are in the early-ish twenty-first century, the Jack for all seasons, the Jackie for all seasons. The Jack of all time, for all time.

It's kismet, baby.

FORGE SOMETHING NEW

Here are one or two thoughts, since all so-called self-help books try to give you at least a gentle nudge in a better direction, if you need one.

We JOATs are everywhere. We are the people you never read about, the people you never hear about. In sports and the arts, the masters deliver the product and we JOATs, we fans and audience members consume it, and find wonder and delight in it. In our work, it's a different story, a different dynamic, but we're still the silent majority. That doesn't mean we aren't happy, or unfulfilled.

We are all unique, every one of us. We each have our own Unique Selling Proposition, our USP. That USP is the special combination of the trades we have and use to our advantage. We can become the ace of trades.

It seems strange that 'what do you want to do in life?' is always phrased as a career question rather than a family or free time question. It should apply to all elements, taken as a whole. As you consider the question for your life as a whole, don't be afraid to forge something new. The key is to forge something new that synthesises the things you do pretty well.

Jack is back. He's never really been away.

my current wife

When it comes to life partners, you never hear someone introduced as 'this is David, my current husband,' unless spoken in jest and with a fair level of mutual understanding and trust between the couple.

This is a different story for the careers we plot, since in this generation we may be married to several jobs before we hang up our working boots for the last time.

Who is my current wife, work-wise? I consider myself to be in a very good position right now, good enough that I have the time and the frame of mind to pen this book.

I work as a business-to-business sales and marketing consultant. I have a long-term contract with a software company that forms the backbone of my work. It takes up most of my week yet gives me sufficient time to slot in other charitable, voluntary and fee-earning projects.

My client likes me because I produce reliable, high quality stuff in the projects I take on. I make it easy to work with me. I am organised, customer focused and thoughtful. I'm fun to work with and because I'm not sucked into office disruptions and politics I work quickly and productively.

In return I get to work from home some of the time, and am around for my kids before and after school. The rest of the time I get to work in client offices which happen to be relatively close to where my mother, brothers and their respective families live.

My current situation reeks of a JOAT approach. This is not surprising, since I've had decades of practice learning what makes me tick and finding the work-life balance that fits the ticking.

Of course, by the time you read this my current work wife and I may have parted company. Nothing lasts forever, fortunately.

"Beautiful Wife B-W (1 of 1)" by mrarmstrong is licensed under CC BY 2.0

Quem tem jeito para tudo, não tem jeito para nada

("He who is good at everything, is good at nothing")

Portuguese

keeping concentration

For the JOAT, it's all about balance. And sometimes, it can feel like a very fine balance. And when I write fine I mean narrow-margined, as opposed to great.

We have a lot of things going on, and a lot of things to stay good at. For this reason, we need to stay focused, stay in the moment, and stay the course. Easy for me to say, right?

JOATs need to be self-aware and constantly monitor how we're doing. It's important for us to maintain our intensity at what we do, and keep our concentration, otherwise we descend into mediocrity. We're a jack of all trades; we don't want to get the reputation of being a jackass at some of them.

The one danger area that JOATs need to stay clear of is flitting between projects, like a small child touching every bun on the plate. This is not the same as having a number of projects running at the same time, nor is it the same as preferring to take projects on sequentially so as to minimise overlap and blurred lines.

To flit between our activities like a butterfly is to not see through a particular phase or chapter of something. It's abandoning a half-done phase because it's easier to start something else. It's being indecisive and not committing to what's important. It's taking the path of least resistance, even though we know that resistance produces friction, electricity, and energy.

I'm not arguing here that we shouldn't have downtime. Breaks and levity are essential parts of our balance, key to us staying productive and catching our breath. But when we're creating we need to knuckle down and not get distracted.

"Butterfly" by Ben124. is licensed under CC BY 2.0

THE SELF-FULFILLING PROPHECY

They say you should write about what you know, but am I right about what I know? I am a JOAT, certainly. When someone examines what I've done for the last few decades, they might be tempted to think, "wow, that lad's done a bit of everything." Another person might draw the conclusion, "hmm, he doesn't appear to have really stuck at anything." You see, it's a question of perspective, how you yourself view the JOAT. Is it everything or anything? This is the yin and yang of the JOAT.

So, it's time we addressed the elephant in the room. "If you can do many things reasonably well, it follows that you're a reasonably good writer. Isn't this book, therefore, only a reasonably good book? Is it good enough to make a difference?" It is perhaps a contradiction in terms that a self-confessed JOAT is professing to be a master of the subject at the same time. It's also a touch ironic that the JOAT can also publish a book, but such is the leveraging power of the media and the web. You can all publish a book, and maybe many of you have.

In many cases, our expectations about something can strongly influence and even govern how it actually turns out, reinforcing those expectations which might have been wrong in the first place. What's your expectation about this book? More importantly, what's your expectation about yourself? Most importantly, what's your expectation about yourself after reading this book? How will you, the JOAT, think about yourself as a result of the content held within these pages?

WHY IT'S GREAT WORKING FOR A JOAT

What's it like working for a JOAT? Someone who knows enough to be dangerous in many areas, yet more than enough to see the danger? Here are some reasons why, if you have a JOAT for a boss, you should be glad:

- a JOAT will admit freely that they're not a master in the subject. They know what the business needs, they know the objectives, but they're happy for you to recommend how to get there
- a JOAT will take a balanced approach to managing you. They won't 'micro-manage' you, emptying your metaphorical ash tray between drags of your cigarette. They won't take a 'command and control' approach, telling you what to do, when to do it and how. They will find the balance between letting you get on with it and providing guidance where necessary
- a JOAT will delegate where they can, and give you responsibility early, knowing that it's not responsibility you're afraid of, it's the more common sibling of accountability without responsibility. They understand that you're not going to grow into your role, make a contribution to the business and improve the way things are done unless you're given a chance to do it yourself, make mistakes and do things better
- a JOAT will always be pushing you to be your best, to do the best you can in the time available. They'll push you in a way that doesn't give you an excuse, or an 'out' if things don't turn out the way you were hoping. They want you to get through as much as you can rather than rework and fine-tune things endlessly to fill the time available

"August 25, 2013" by osseous is licensed under CC BY 2.0

sales versus marketing

Sales and marketing are supposed to go together like bread and butter, but they often end up being like chalk and cheese. In the business-to-business world a lot is made of the need for sales and marketing to work well together, since what marketing tries to start, sales tries to finish. Yet what you tend to see is a gulf between the two camps. Differences in alignment, objectives, preferences, and – crucially – perspectives.

My own view of sales and marketing being uneasy bedfellows is that – and I'm having to generalise here, with no pun intended – sales tends to be a more specialist role, requiring more depth in a narrower set of skills, whereas marketing tends to be more generalist, demanding a broader array of competencies.

I was reminded of this fact during the course of writing this book, when pursuing two great job opportunities with two great software companies looking to take their business to the next level. I have a lot of experience in both sales and marketing, with the balance being weighted probably 70-to-30 in favour of marketing. The key point here is not that I was a better fit for the marketing role, but that I was more nervous about concentrating on the small number of specific things that the sales role demanded. 'Develop the people, hit the sales targets, hire more people, develop them, hit higher sales targets, rinse and repeat.'

The marketing remit was broader, needing a command of more areas to help put the sales teams in the best possible position. I felt more comfortable with the role. The upshot of the interview process? I was offered the marketing role, and not the sales role.

Bun la toate și la nimic

("Good at everything and at nothing")

Romanian

"Romanian Painters - Tonitza" by dorinsb is licensed under CC BY 2.0

surrounded by greatness

'Great' is literally a great word isn't it? Great and greatness are qualities to aspire to. Great connotes size and importance, leadership and a lasting quality. There's the famous quote that some are born great, while some have greatness thrust upon them. It's either the accident of birth or being the right person, in the right place, at the right time. It seems like greatness equals being a master of something.

Sometimes as JOATs we feel like we're surrounded by greatness. Not always physically surrounded, but also virtually, via our television, radio, laptop or mobile device, in the office or the living room. "He's great at that, she's great at something else, and that one is the greatest, full stop. I can do many of those things, and even if I haven't done them I bet I could do them, but not as well as that person is doing that one thing."

Of course, we could all write a screenplay, play for England, lead the country, run Pepsi. But would we be any good? Would we be good enough? Would we be great? No, of course not. And how would we bypass the years of dedication and the thinnest of bottlenecks between our armchair and the real field of battle?

We're not focused on being great. We're focused on being greater than we are now, greater than we were yesterday. More importantly, we're focused on the greater good of mankind. We like to level the playing field wherever we can, to give everyone a fair shot at greatness. We believe in the ideal world of the meritocracy, in which you achieve what you deserve. And that, in itself, is great.

"Girt by Sea" by mikecogh is licensed under CC BY-SA 2.0

Here is the paradox and the contradiction within the concept of the Jack of All Trades and the Master of None, between the generalist and the specialist.

There is no one JOAT.

the JOAT paradox

Yet we are all JOATs, or at least the overwhelming majority of us. We are the same yet different, as the make-up of our trades varies within each of us.

You see, Jack of All Trades or Master of One is, to all practical purposes, a binary thing. You're either in the well-known 1% or in the unknown 99%, yet there's an almost infinite range of generalist capabilities within the 99%.

It's a question of degree. How much of a JOAT are you? You could be the Jack of All Trades, the Jack of Some Trades, the Super Jack of Two or Three Trades.

You could also be the Jack within a highly specialist niche. That's the thing: if you narrow it down enough, you are among the best at what you do. The one true specialist, the king or queen of your market of one.

Sounds heretical, but it's true.

Happy
Darwin
Day

the evolutionary JOAT

If the JOAT is in the large middle of the pack in many things, why haven't we evolved away into nothing? If it's the fittest that survive, why are there so many of us?

Perhaps the JOAT is born of modern society. Would we have survived in pre-civilised times when specialist fighters, craftsmen and legislators ruled the day? Throughout the ages there have been armies to fight wars. In each army there are great fighters and average fighters. Stellar fighters kill journeyman fighters, armies get steadily better over time. A rising tide lifts all boats, right? This analogy falls down because fallen fighters get replaced by more fighters, most of whom will be good fighters and only a few of whom will be the very best.

It turns out that it's not the best that survive and evolve, it's the most adaptable. Who's the most adaptable? You are of course. You've spent your life adapting to new things, acquiring new skills, learning new things and moving with the times. Adapting is what you do, all the time. Up here for thinking, down there for dancing.

You are the fittest, in both senses of the word.

the sporting microcosm

My sporting experience is a microcosm of my overall joatness. I've chosen to divide my decades of work and leisure into a number of pursuits, and I've gotten to be decent at them. This allows me to vary my activities and still get a good degree of quality output and enjoyment out of them all.

Even within the areas I choose to give limited time to, I find myself generalising rather than specialising. At football, most players are predominantly one-footed. They favour that foot and will almost always move the ball to it, pass with it and shoot with it. This makes them very good on that one foot, but it also makes them predictable. I have always worked on my left foot as much as my right, and while I'm pretty right-sided and can kick harder with the right foot, I'm equally confident using the left foot. This makes it harder to defend against me.

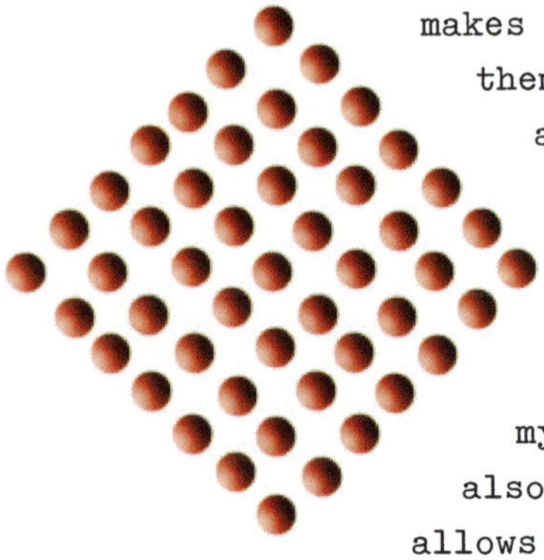

When I played a lot of table tennis, I decided that my backhand was not as strong as my forehand. This is also true of the majority of players, since the forehand allows us a much bigger swing path so you can hit the ball harder. I spent a year practising my backhand more than my left, and I became equally proficient on both sides. I no longer had to make allowances and cover for weaknesses in my game.

When I played cricket, I wasn't the fastest bowler, I was medium pace, so I generally came on at the first bowling change. I wasn't the best batsman, but I was solid, so I batted in the middle of the order. In the field, I prided myself on being able to field anywhere, from the slips to the ropes.

My ability to generalise within a specific sport and career path gave me an edge, and a look that was different from the fastest, the biggest, the strongest, the brightest, or the beautifulest.

За десять дел возьмется, ни одно не закончит

("Starts ten things, finishes none")

Russian

"Unfinished house, c1913" by crackdog is licensed under CC BY 2.0

surviving today's economy

For some time the landscape of some national economies has been shifting. The largest companies have been contracting and the volume of smaller companies has been growing. Automation will continue to supplant humans in many jobs, with the exception of professions like teaching and caring.

These days anyone can be an entrepreneur, setting themselves up in business, in more control of their choices, their destiny, and their wellbeing. That's great news for us, because JOATs are very well suited to entrepreneurial demands. We can do lots of things fairly well, a vital feather in our cap when we're responsible for so many different areas of the business.

Just think about the three most important things a CEO has to do in the business. First, as its Chief 'Culture' Officer, they have to articulate the values and vision of the company, banging the drum with a consistent message. Second, they need to hire the best very talent they can get in each role in the business. Third, they're responsible for securing the finances of the company, staying on top of cash flow and making sure the business can make its obligations to its stakeholders. That's a pretty diverse remit, don't you think? Something you could handle with your basket of skills? I thought so.

Specialists and specialities? They belong in larger companies, the big machines that need a specific shaped and sized cog to do a specific job.

Right now has never been a better time for the JOAT. You can do a bunch of things and still make your family, your life and your finances hum.

THE SUPERLATIVE

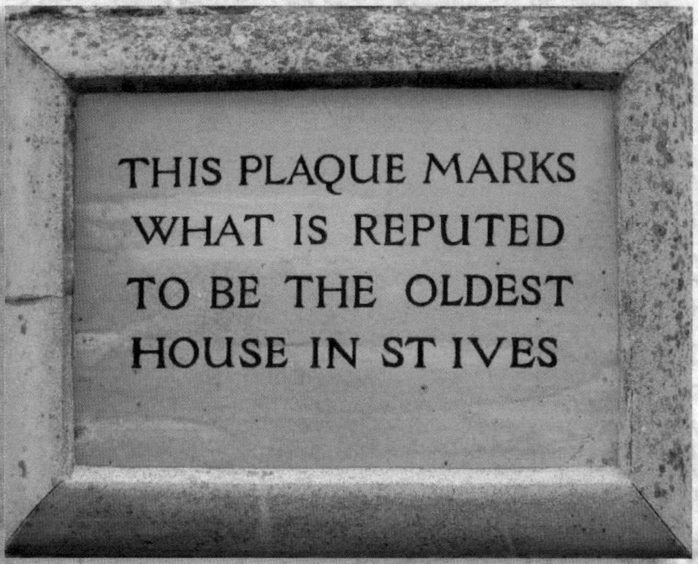

"Reputed to be..." by dipfan is licensed under CC BY 2.0

In language we distinguish three types of adjective. These are the positive, comparative and superlative. 'Good' is the positive. 'Better' is the comparative, since you're comparing the two things, people or groups. "I was the better fighter." "The reds are better than the blues." 'Best' is the superlative, the top dog. No-one's better than the best.

If you experienced the crazy, nonsensical days of the dot com boom around the turn of the last century, you'll remember that sense of trying to move as fast as you possibly could. It was like a land-grab situation from the Klondyke Gold Rush era. The prevailing mantra at the time was "ready, fire, aim".

Now, however, business is focused on the superlative. It's not enough to be good enough. It's not enough to be better than the rest. It's got to be the best. Business bosses beg for the superlative. If it's not perfect, rework it until it is. In some industries like 'med tech', with their '6 sigma' focus on quality, this is understandable. Medical devices have to be perfect. You can't have a faulty stent; the downside is very bleak for the end customer. In most other industries, perfect is simply not necessary.

The superlative does not sit well with the JOAT, most of whose prodigious output is better, but rarely the best. The superlative is specialist territory, and we don't venture there. It's far better for the JOAT to realise that 99% of the time, perfect doesn't exist. When you've done your best, it's ready to go, so submit it, get it out there. Then you can move on to the next thing.

THE TALENT TRAP

In recent years, coaches, mentors and other deep thinkers have eschewed the argument that talent trumps effort and set about creating the correct environment for world-beating success. They've focused on good coaching, good facilities and access to both so that the neophytes can amass the thousands of hours they need to get the millions of repetitions under their belt. With repetition comes muscle memory, so that the truly great can rely on the moving parts doing their job faultlessly as the brain is completely engaged, in the moment and making the split-second decisions that divide winning and losing.

The notion that great champions are made not born is

bolstered by the fact that the greatest exponents in their field have always practised. Practice, practice, practice, refining their art, every waking second if they possibly could. I think this is a fair argument, but I also think we can't completely discount the importance of natural talent. Our genetic make-up pre-disposes us to certain types of skills, certain types of activities, certain types of jobs. If we displayed any kind of talent in our early days, before we'd even started to accumulate the practice time, we were spotted and singled out for further coaching.

Our early talent at things also brought us success, which in turn brought happiness and the will to repeat that happiness, thereby completing the virtuous circle. Talent is important, as is practice, mental fortitude, and occasional slices of good fortune. As JOATs, our preference is to divide that talent, and the corresponding effort, in a number of directions. The end result gives us pleasure, but it doesn't give pleasure to thousands or millions of others.

blueprint of a generalist

When I look back on my own business career to date, I see a pattern of variety, adaptability and breadth.

- I've spent time marketing selling, and selling marketing. I've sold marketing services like creativity and branding, and I've marketed sales improvement and effectiveness
- I've worked for micro-companies (one-to-six staff), small businesses (seven-to-a-hundred staff), medium-sized companies (a-hundred-to-a-thousand staff) and large companies (more than a thousand staff)
- I've worked for clients in the public sector – local government, semi-states, Non-Governmental Organisations, charitable organisations – and for clients in the private sector, across a range of industries
- I've worked in an agency providing marketing services to customers, and as a customer commissioning and managing marketing services and suppliers
- I've been an employee, a contractor, a consultant, a volunteer, a director and a trustee
- I've worked at home and abroad
- I've worked for software companies serving different industries: insurance, security, marketing, sales, security, IT, ecommerce, sourcing and procurement
- I've worked across the sales and marketing spectrum
- I've done loads of business-to-business and a little business-to-consumer

What does this give me?

- An informed perspective on a lot of things, born of experience and of having made mistakes
- Ideas, methods and success stories that can transfer and cross-fertilise in different industries
- The ability to anticipate, adapt, accelerate and add value, almost anywhere

Quien mucho abarca poco aprieta

("He who embraces too much, has a weak grasp")
Spanish

THERE CAN BE ONLY ONE

There can be only one regional champion, one national champion, one world champion. There can be only one team leader, one head of department, one chief executive. There can only be one political head of a region, one leader of the political party, one leader of the country. There can only be one winner of the prize, whatever that prize is.

Maybe you won prizes at something, and then you went on to the next level. Maybe you won prizes at that level too. At some point you start to analyse how you measured up against the people at the next level. At some point it gets serious. Really serious. At some point you come up against people for whom it's always been serious. And it's not fun anymore. You might come second, or worse. For there can be only one.

To take a line from Max Ehrmann's Desiderata: "If you compare yourself with others, you may become vain and bitter; for always there will be greater and lesser persons than yourself." Vanity and bitterness is for those who are competing with others, for those who are specialists – or believe they are specialists – in whatever they do.

You should be competing with yourself. This is why our teachers, coaches and other bodies encourage us to be the best we can be, to do our best, to better ourselves. There's nothing wrong with all of us striving to be the best, as long as we understand that it's our best that counts. This way we avoid unhealthy, unproductive feelings like vanity and bitterness.

The natural inclination of the JOAT is to go wide. The more things we do, the more things we can call skills, the more options we have, the more marketable that makes us. Yes, all good, to a point.

Remember that there's only one of you, though. You can't clone yourself – yet. You can't do everything pretty well. You can't even do almost everything pretty well. There's simply not enough time to develop the skills, earn the experience and make the mistakes. With every additional skill you add or claim, you experience decreasing marginal returns, which means you're damaging your productivity.

You are not jam. Don't spread yourself too thin. You need to devote enough time to your trades in order to stay a jack at them. Too many trades and you can't do this. The specialists do one thing really, really well. The dilettantes, the tyre-kickers and fly-by-nights have a go at everything and stick at nothing. The generalists do a few things rather well and combine them in ways that bring something new and in situations that call for a blended approach.

Again, it's all about balance and finding the right number of trades you can stay good at. This depends, of course, on how narrowly you define your trade, and how well your discrete trades dovetail to create your unique offering to the world. My advice is to think about 'bullet points on a slide'. You want at least three, but no more than seven. Each bullet point needs to be big enough, and striking enough, to make a difference.

you are not jam

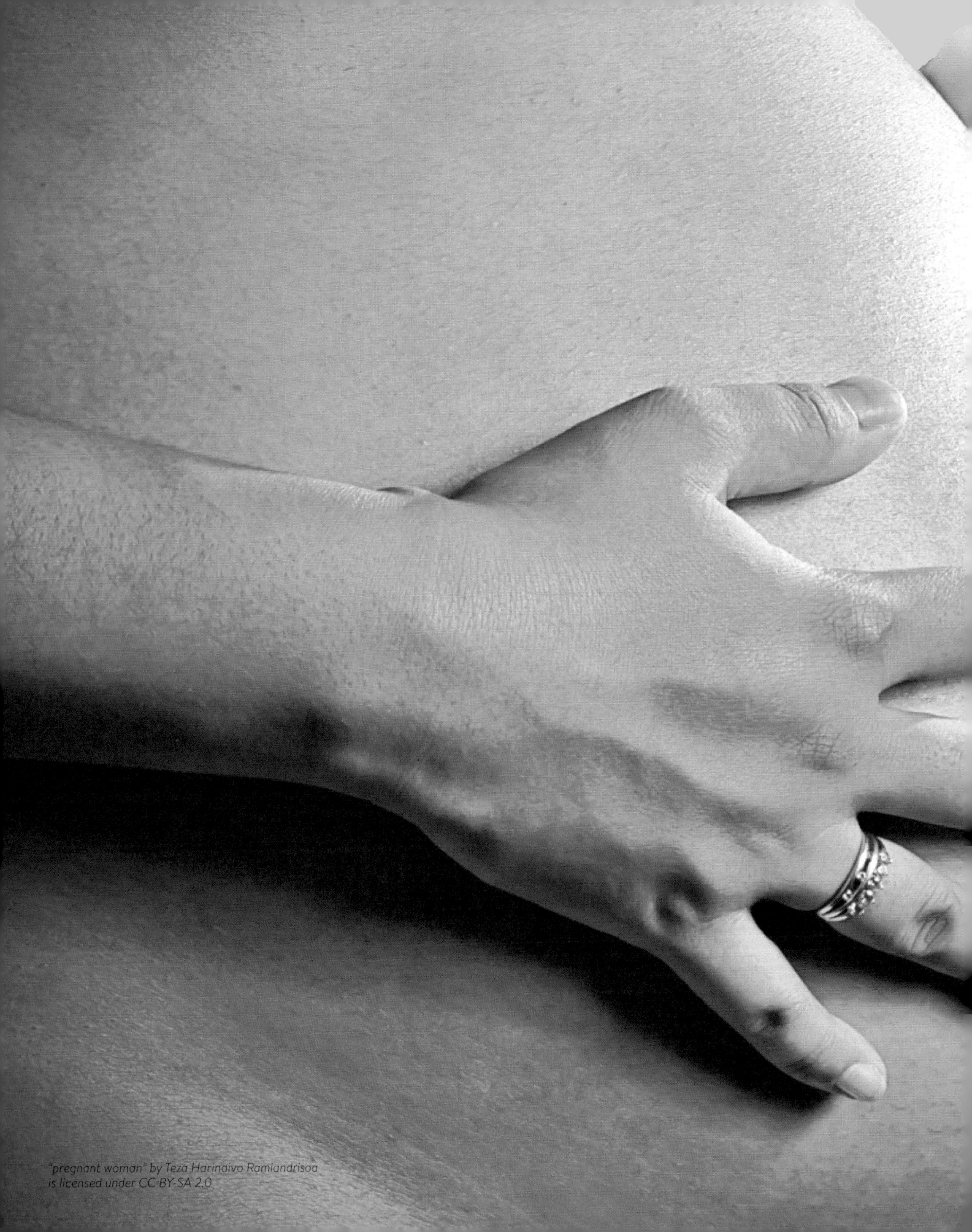

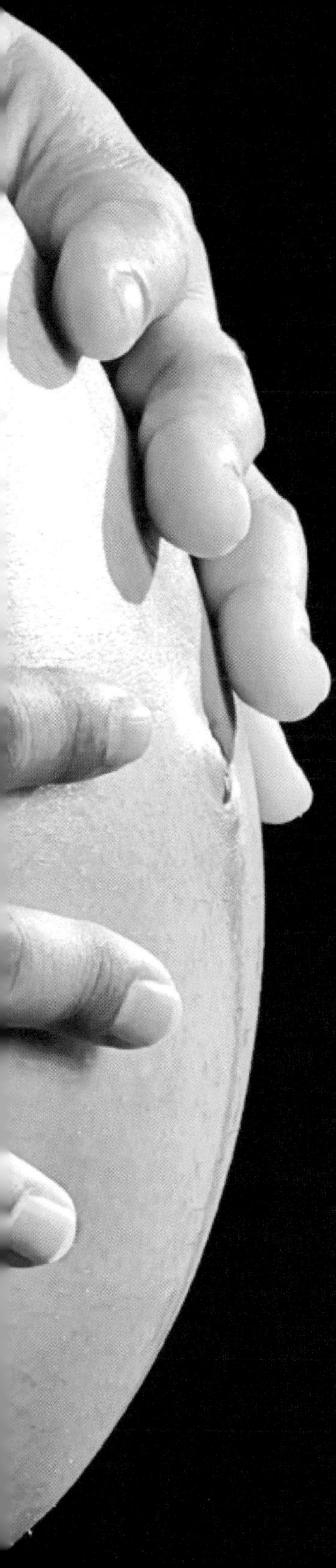

the JOAT parent

There isn't much of a job description for being a parent, and there's not much training either. We pretty much get dropped into one of the most demanding and diverse jobs you can imagine. It's a full-time job being a dresser, washer, teacher, funder, protector, feeder, carer, advisor.

Yet, when you think about it, JOATs make great parents. Think of all the different skills we need to acquire. Think of all the different phases a child goes through in its upbringing, the steep learning curves and the hurtling emotions of the rollercoaster. Each phase presents a different set of challenges for them and us and each requires a different mix of those parenting skills than before.

If you're a parent and a JOAT, you're bringing into the world a child that may not end up in the 1%. It may not end up being a specialist. In that case the chances are the child doesn't know what it wants to do in life, nor may it ever find out during its whole life. Our vital role as a parent is to expose our children to as many different experiences as we possibly can, to see which ones stick. It sounds pretty daunting, but then again, there's no better role model than us for the multi-faceted life well lived, is there?

Specialists are so caught up in and committed to being the best that they tend to get other people to bring up their kids for them. They don't have the time, or they don't make the time, or they're not around. Which sounds best for the child to you?

writing this book

As I mentioned near the beginning of this book, I laboured over the best structure for it. Normally, I like to start with a beginning and an end, before working on an outline framework for how the book will flow – and hopefully glow – from one end to the other.

This book wasn't normal. There's very little written on the subject, which seems alarming given the amount of people it caters to. It's either an unbelievable oversight by society at large – or by me. There was, therefore, no set format to consider, which suited me fine.
What I had was a sense there was a story worth writing and a collection of thoughts that, when taken together, didn't help me with the final chapter where I could tell how it would turn out. I had a few ideas for themes that would hold the story together, and liked them all.

Against my normal way of doing things I started writing and filling out my thoughts into coherent, digestible chunks of what I thought was important. The more I worked on the book, the more I became friends with the notion that I could use all the themes and the book would be the richer for it.

You will by now have recognised this as the latest milestone – and in fact the last that I will share with you as it brings us right up to the here and now – in the life of an irrepressible JOAT. Hedging bets, seeking out variety, risking compromise – all the main threads of the JOAT personality are there.

பல தொழில் கற்றவன் ஒரு தொழிலும் செய்யான்

("A man who has learnt many businesses will do none")

Tamil

it is what it is

So, you're a JOAT. You know this now. Perhaps you've suspected it for a long time. Maybe you've known it all along.

Relax. It is what it is. What it is hasn't been written about much, if at all. A mixed make-up of skills and facilities is what characterises most people, yet where is the help, the support structure to help you understand your 'condition' and become your best? No matter. You know the secret now, and you have the key to unlock it.

You have your own JUSP, your own JOAT Unique Selling Proposition. It's the unique blend of what you do well that you can offer to people and help them get to where they need to be. What could be more generous than that? And you get to grow too, into the bargain.

You are a joatastic individual. Gaze upon the joatorama of opportunities that present themselves to you. Select the one that offers the best fit to your special bundle of trades and pursue it with vitality. Revel in your own unique joatage. Celebrate it.

you need a pack, jack

Whether it's looking for a new job, or a new venture of your own, or a new idea for your free time and the free time of your family, you have to package your plan. Even if it's just an outline plan, with some timelines, it sets up the runway for you and gives you something to aim for.

We all know those people who have fallen into new careers, new jobs, or new pastimes. Plenty of JOATS have acquired their portfolio of experiences this way. A chance meeting, a casual conversation, an accidental connection. But once the trigger is pulled, once you get the catalyst that nudges you into forward motion, you need a plan to follow through on the spark. Your Jack-pack needs to help you through these eight questions:

What am I looking to do?

Who am I looking to do it for?

What are the bits that make up what I'm looking to do?

Why am I looking to do it?

Where am I looking to do it?

How am I looking to do it?

When am I looking to do it by?

Who am I looking to for help to do it?

"Swirling Tangles" by garlandcannon is licensed under CC BY 2.0

Your pack is not an inanimate object gathering dust. It's a living, breathing thing, a proxy for a short period of your life. Some folks scribble notes in a stream of consciousness. Some do a spreadsheet. Some make a list. Some draw a map. Some do it in their head. Whatever your approach, make a plan, follow a plan, adapt a plan.

the consulting conundrum

As I write this book, I've enjoyed the longest sustained period of consulting in my career so far. I live in a lovely part of the world, and many people I know have realised that in order to stay living here, with a decent standard of living, they had to start their own business. Mine happens to be a consulting business, which 95% of the time is me and me alone, but if I get the right idea to start a tech company, I will certainly try that too.

You would think that a consulting practice is about as specialised as it's possible to get. After all, people are paying you for your specific expertise. In my experience, though, this is not the case. First of all, you are a business advisor and so you're often called upon to deliver advice across the business spectrum. Second, you get to work with different companies from different industries, and this widens your experience base very quickly. Third, you get to do work that is not only in your wheelhouse but also complementary to it and outside of it.

Over the last dozen or so years, I have helped companies find the right international ad agency partner, been an interim CMO, provided sales management expertise, run product feasibility projects, managed product launches, done product marketing, sales enablement and demand generation campaigns, and created hundreds of thousands of words of compelling content. I also provide mentoring advice to small businesses looking to accelerate their growth.

There it is, the portfolio career. Tailored specifically, to you, the generalist

Một nghề cho chín, còn hơn chín nghề

("Being master in one job is better than being average in nine jobs")

Vietnamese

the big seven

1. You are a JOAT. JOAT is not a dirty word. Being a JOAT sets you up in the best way to adapt to the viciously quick vagaries of the modern world. If you're made up this way, you should be made up.

2. Be happy, knowing that you've got natural balance in your work and life and that you can spread that happiness and make a difference to others. Not for you the pain of the tortured artiste or the monotony of the one-track mind.

3. Understand that being a JOAT is not a crutch to lean on, an excuse for not being your best, or a justification to embrace mediocrity. You are as driven as the master of one trade, but you dance to a different tune, knowing that the sum of your parts is greater than your whole.

4. You are in control, control of your work/life balance, your options, your choices and your time. The breadth of things you do well gives you the control, the flexibility and the freedom to grow – indefinitely.

5. Happy with your lot? Keep doing what you're doing. If it's working for you, and those that matter to you, don't change a thing, but keep an eye out and be ready for things that might upset your hard-earned equilibrium.

6. Want to be a better JOAT, maybe an ace of trades? Ruthlessly weed out the trades that you're not really a jack of. Look for or create opportunities that combine your unique mix of the things you're good at.

7. Want to be a master of one trade, a true specialist? First, be sure such a thing exists in your field, and it's attainable. Second, make a plan and pursue your goal relentlessly, single-mindedly, fearlessly

THIS MUCH I KNOW

this much I know

This book is – literally – this much I know. It is the accumulated experiences that I carry in my head, that I've organised and put between the covers of this book.

I've done very little research for this book. I didn't refer back to any old diaries or documented evidence. As much as anything it's a demonstration to me that what I've done so far has both variety and value and that I remember enough of it to inform and colour whatever I do next.

I hope it gives you a nudge to write your own story. We've enough stories from the 1%. It's time to start tipping the balance in favour of the 99%. What we have to say about ourselves is more useful to the rest of us.

credits & sources

I credit every picture individually using the Creative Commons licensing codes. My undying thanks are to those who put their work out there for the rest of us to share.

All language versions of the phrase "Jack of All Trades, Master of None" are from Wikipedia: http://en.wikipedia.org/wiki/Jack_of_all_trades,_master_of_none

Wikipedia is a miracle of modern times, an enormous work of generosity, and a non-profit organisation. Go here to donate: http://wikimediafoundation.org/wiki/Ways_to_Give

acknowledgements & dedication

I would like to thank my wife for her unstinting support in all that is important, her conscious ignorance of all that is not, and her smarts to make the distinction.

My kids have weathered the withering winds of me being around far too much and who have declared themselves satisfied by my inadequate answers to the question: 'Dad, when will you be getting a job?' They continually amaze me by being better than me at stuff I think I'm good at.

Designer Sophie Pelham (@ceaupheee) worked miracles with a horrifying array of moving parts and kept her super high quality and irrepressibly good humour.

My good friend and writer Garry Holland has been unfailingly constructive in his feedback and criticism of this work, especially in the early days when it was an amorphous blob composed primarily of intuition and not particularly well thought out ideas.

My brothers, who both found their vocations well before I'll find mine, have been most supportive, and have manfully resisted the urge to rub in the fact that they published books decades before me.

Many agents, editors and publishers saw this book in its unpublished state. They all passed on it, perhaps because they're all specialists and it didn't appeal. Some of them provided great feedback. To those that did, thank you.

Staying in JOAT mode, this book is for me as much about the journey of writing as it is the destination, the matter of doing it for the thrill of the ride and of self-discovery. It took me 50 years to figure it out and to cop on, and so, in a squirming break with protocol I would like to thank myself for having the guts to get on the bus, the tenacity to break the finishing tape with my chest out and the insouciance to mix my metaphors.

Thanks to you too, Jack and Jackie, for bothering to read this bit, unless you're like me and you start from the covers and work your way in, in which case you have much work to do my friends...

Dedicated to my parents, for their dedication to me, and for their combined DNA.

you do know jack!

To all the JOATs out there: sorry it took so long, I had other things to do...

"Open is Never Having to Say You Are Sorry" by cogdogblog is licensed under CC CC0 1.0

Printed in Poland
by Amazon Fulfillment
Poland Sp. z o.o., Wrocław

58024805R00093